access to geography

SPORT *and* LEISURE

Stuart Terrell

Hodder & Stoughton

A MEMBER OF THE HODDER HEADLINE GROUP

Dedication: For Ian, Iris and Laura.

The author would like to thank Luke Wilson, whose own research
as an A2 student helped in the writing of this book.

Acknowledgements

The publishers would like to thank the following individuals, institutions and
companies for permission to reproduce copyright illustrations in this book:

Reproduced by permission of Ordnance Survey on behalf of The Controller of Her
Majesty's Stationery Office, © Crown Copyright 100036470, page 64.

Every effort has been made to trace and acknowledge ownership of copyright. The publishers will be glad to make suitable arrangements with any copyright holders whom it
has not been possible to contact.

Note about the Internet links in the book. The user should be aware that URLs or web
addresses change regularly. Every effort has been made to ensure the accuracy of the
URLs provided in this book on going to press. It is inevitable, however, that some will
change. It is sometimes possible to find a relocated web page, by just typing in the
address of the home page for a website in the URL window of your browser.

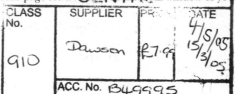

Orders: please contact Bookpoint Ltd, 130 Milton Park, Abingdon, Oxon OX14 4SB.
Telephone: (44) 01235 827720. Fax: (44) 01235 400454. Lines are open from
9.00 to 6.00, Monday to Saturday, with a 24 hour message answering service. You can
also order through our website www.hodderheadline.co.uk.

British Library Cataloguing in Publication Data
A catalogue record for this title is available from the British Library

ISBN 0 340 81501 9

First Published 2004
Impression number 10 9 8 7 6 5 4 3 2 1
Year   2010 2009 2008 2007 2006 2005 2004

Cover photo: ActionPlus/Neil Tingle
Produced by Gray Publishing, Tunbridge Wells, Kent
Printed in Malta for Hodder & Stoughton Educational, a division of
Hodder Headline, 338 Euston Road, London NW1 3BH.

Contents

1 Sport and Leisure Perspectives and the Growth of Sport and Leisure

KEY WORDS

Sport: all forms of physical activity that, through casual or organised participation, aim at improving physical fitness and mental well being, forming social relationships, or obtaining results in competitions at all levels
Leisure: relatively freely chosen activity and experience that takes place in time free from work and other obligations
Figurational sociology: study of human behaviour through the interdependent relationships formed via networks or 'figurations' of people
Civilising process: the application of figurational sociology, whereby society's changes in values is reflected in its leisure forms
Recreation: leisure time activity that does not take place within a formal setting of rules and that may or may not involve travel away from home
Work: all forms of obligated activity, both paid and unpaid, formal or informal

Sport and leisure are key factors in today's society. No matter who we are, or what our status is, one or both of these will have a bearing on the way we live our lives. Sport and leisure hold different meanings for different people, and it is hard to produce a definition on which all will agree. This chapter aims to address this, and attempts to produce a general idea that is easy to understand, and that covers all aspects of both sport and leisure.

1 Sport and Leisure Perspectives

a) Defining sport

The definition of sport given above is a concise version from the Council of Europe's *European Sports Charter*, adopted in 1992, and based on their earlier (and much wordier) attempt at a definition in 1980, which splits sport into four categories:

- competitive games/sports accepting rules and characterised by responses to opposing challenges

- outdoor pursuits where participants seek to negotiate some form of terrain. Challenges are derived from type of terrain (water, mountain, forest, sky, etc.), weather conditions and mode of negotiation
- aesthetic movements including activities that create delight in the pleasure of patterned body movements, e.g. figure skating, dance, recreational swimming
- conditioning activity, such as exercise, used to improve physical ability.

(Adapted from *Council for Europe 1980*, in Gratton and Taylor, 2000.)

However, definitions differ around the world. The North American idea of sport, for example, is of competition, following specific rules – anything else is defined as **recreation** (see the Key Words on p. 1). This attempt at distinction can cause problems, not least when you attempt to define a recognisable activity as sport. Figure 1 shows the continuum of cricket – from the extreme of French cricket, all the way to test matches.

Many people may consider that cricket, in whatever form it is played, is a sport. However, purists may argue that it does not become a sport until you reach the more formal variation, from club cricket in this case.

Recreation			Sport
French cricket: no defined boundaries, no teams.	**Garden/beach cricket:** no teams, but vague attempt to formalise area. Teams optional.	**Club cricket:** formalised rules and boundary, variable quality. Teams selected.	**First-class cricket:** formal rules, high-quality facilities. Professionalism.

Figure 1 A continuum to show examples of the different levels at which cricket may be played.

b) Defining leisure

If sport was hard to define, leisure is doubly so. Over the years, academics have argued over the many different ways in which it can be represented. For example, one widely accepted theory was put forward by Haywood *et al.* (1995) in their **four dimensions of leisure**. As shown in Table 1, these perceptions are still open to criticism. Their approach was to break down leisure into its fundamental components, and into the most basic perceptions, to try and explain patterns of leisure through the behaviour of individuals in their non-work time. Each of these viewpoints on leisure has its advantages and disadvantages, but it should be up to the student to determine which they favour. Within the context of this book, a combination of dimensions 1 and 4 has been used to formulate the definition at the beginning of this chapter. Leisure can best be defined by assuming that

Table 1   Dimensions of leisure (after Haywood *et al.*, 1995)

Dimension: leisure as...	Strength	Weakness
Residual time	Simple to calculate for those in *paid* employment Comparisons easy to make over time and between occupations and countries	Difficult to calculate for unpaid work, e.g. homemakers, unemployed Large section of population therefore ignored
Activity	Easy to understand: common sense way of thinking about leisure	Ignores passive leisure. Uncertain status of activities such as religion, do-it-yourself, charity work Difficult to calculate for certain groups, e.g. professional artists, sports professionals
Function	Focuses on content and social consequences of leisure	Does not necessarily discriminate between leisure and other activities Sees leisure as utilitarian; ignores unjustified fun
Freedom	Focuses on subjective value of leisure, on the quality of leisure experience Identifies activities that have been historically valued as leisure	Hard to quantify; some activities have multiple motivations May not distinguish leisure from work and other obligations

non-work time is leisure time, although this then assumes there is a paid or obligated time from which to be free. Whether it be walking the dog, watching television, swimming or sleeping, such activities can be considered as leisure. Whether they fall under any other umbrella depends on how formal, active or passive the use of that time is.

The viewpoints in Table 1 are very modern constructs. Leisure itself, as a subject of academic study, is a late arrival to societal theories; previous sociological theories had concentrated on work, politics, family and the organisation of society as a whole. It had always been considered to be peripheral and unimportant. As a result, there has been little discussion of leisure time in history, and what has been said tends to be superficial.

Two other authors were concerned about the lack of importance placed on what is now seen as a critical area of study in sociology. Norbert Elias developed 'figurational sociology', a concept whereby networks of interdependencies are created between individuals, and their actions invariably have a knock-on effect throughout the rest of network (or figuration). Eric Dunning extended Elias' ideas to sport, seeing a team as a figuration in itself, whereby the actions of one team member dictated the way in which others behaved, including the opposing figuration. This theory, while useful, developed further into what these authors called the 'civilising process', a concept whereby human leisure develops in a similar way to society. This will be studied in greater detail later in this chapter.

Leisure theories not only look at what leisure is, but also how it is carried out, and what importance it holds in everyday life. For example, the perspectives of leisure shown in Figure 2 may well link closely to the type of society in which one lives, and the opportunities one has for leisure. From the 1950s onwards, and into the 1990s in particular, in the UK, new leisure patterns emerged as society developed in such a way that leisure time increased markedly, due to:

- an increasing number of part-time jobs
- increased amount of job-sharing
- increasing self-employment.

As a result, leisure lifestyles developed within a framework in which everyone could be placed, no matter how diverse their leisure experience. This included the **frequency** and **number of activities** in which they took part (see Figure 2).

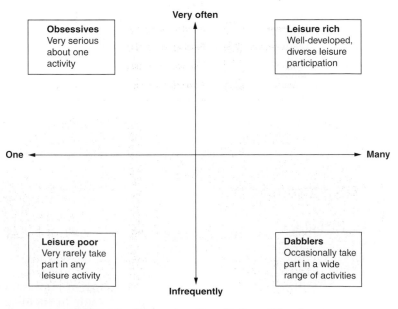

Figure 2 Dimensionality of leisure lifestyles.

c) Defining recreation

As already indicated, recreation is a term closely associated with leisure, but one that assumes a particular activity is being performed. If you like, leisure can be seen as the *time* free from work, and recreation what is *done* with that time. Therefore, it could perhaps be seen as formalising what is done with leisure time.

2 Sport, Leisure, Recreation and Work Relationships

Figure 3 gives some idea of *one* perception of the interaction of these four demands on our time.

According to the definitions given, recreation must be a full part of leisure, as it involves 'leisure time activities'. In this case, recreation attempts to formalise and structure leisure time into specific activities. Sport is both a part of leisure and recreation, and, in the case of professionals, a part of work as well.

There is no definite rule about the exact relationship of these areas. People will inevitably form their own opinions as to what they consider to be sport, leisure and recreation, and within academic

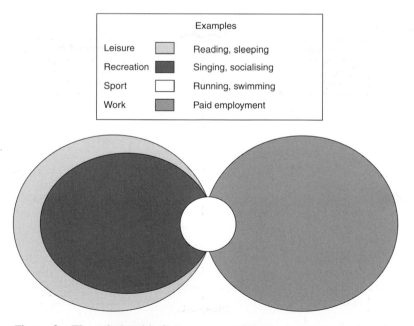

Figure 3   The relationship between sport, leisure, recreation and work.

research, this is desirable, as it means wider reading of other stand-points is required. However, within this book, the assumptions made earlier will be adhered to.

3 Historical Perspectives on the Geography of Sport and Leisure

Sport and leisure in more economically developed countries (MEDCs) owes a great deal to historical precedents that were developed over many centuries, and the concepts and rules of sport and leisure activities were refined alongside the growth of civilisation. The best documented beginnings of sport and leisure can be found in the many writings of the Ancient Greeks, and it is here that the study of the development of modern sport should begin, in the way it spread from the Mediterranean to the whole of the Western world. Table 2 shows a summary of the approximate timescale of the development of sport, from its earliest inception around the Mediterranean area, to the fall of the Roman Empire.

During the period between the Neolithic Revolution and the fall of the Roman Empire, four major sporting cultures existed that had an influence on the development of sports at this time. They were the Minoan culture of the third and second millennia BC, the Mycenaean culture of the second millennium BC, the city-states of Greece in the sixth, fifth and fourth centuries BC, and the Roman society from the first century AD. Most of the information on these cultures is gained from archaeological evidence, and the writings of several prominent writers at the time.

Following through this table, it is also possible to study the early sports in terms of figurational sociology and the civilising process. Elias and Dunning explained that over time, societal norms and values changed, and as small states amalgamated into larger nations, figurations grew longer, and so the need for violence diminished. An example of this can be seen in today's society. Violence is not tolerated in sport and leisure, and sports such as hunting and boxing are often protested against. Yet 50 years ago, these were seen as civilised pastimes. Looking at Table 2, it can be seen that there was a decline in the civilising process in the ancient world, as pastimes became more violent during the Roman Empire, and less concerned with aesthetics, as in the earlier Greek civilisations. Even through the Middle Ages, violent pastimes (bear-baiting, cock-fighting) were common, and sporting pastimes seldom had defined rules. It was not until the growth of public school sports, and the modern Olympic era, that civilisation has approached the kind of sport and leisure ethos associated with Ancient Greece.

Table 2   Timeline of sports development in the ancient world

Before 1000 BC	**'Non-sport' period** Physical activities tied to survival and expression of religious beliefs
900 BC	**Ancient Greek games** Included as parts of festivals, central to religion and mythology Events based on interests of young wealthy males, often including military competitions
550 BC	**'Modern' Greek games** Buildings constructed at Olympia – shrine to Zeus, so kept religious connections Athletes hired or sponsored by states – start of professionalism Seen as an art form
100 BC	**Roman games** Used to train soldiers and entertain masses Used by rulers to maintain authority and control
100 AD	**Roman spectacles** Gladiatorial contests and circuses created Focused on violent sport forms
300 AD	Violence increases – fights to death, vs animals, criminals, Christians, etc.
400 AD	Demise of Roman Empire and its games and spectacles

a) Minoan/Mycenaean cultures

Both of these cultures seemed to run reasonably parallel during the second millennium BC, with the Mycenaean culture taking over from the Minoan during that period. Initially, the Minoan culture dominated the island of Crete, and physical activities such as bull-leaping and dancing, were depicted in ancient frescoes, indicating early sport forms. Minoan culture mostly disappeared around 1500 BC, possibly due to invasions from mainland Greece, and the growing Mycenaean culture.

The best evidence of this culture is gained from the epic poems of the time, such as Homer's *Iliad* and *Odyssey*. Both of these poems are an account of the 'heroic age', were heroes were considered to epitomise all that was desirable, and where the closest humans could get to being gods. Physical prowess of the heroes is the overriding concern in both these poems.

The *Iliad* is based primarily on Mycenaean culture, which mainly encompasses the siege of Troy by Mycenae in the thirteenth century BC. This was an historical event embellished by the introduction of gods and heroes, concentrating mainly on the athletic and military feats of the latter. In fact, there is little mention of anyone else, indicating that physical ability and warfare were now held in greater regard than the more aesthetic activities of the earlier Minoan culture.

During most of this period sporting events had both a religious and military purpose, but there was little formality in terms of sporting contests. Most were seen as small-scale competitions between warriors attempting to assert their physical prowess over their adversary. It was not until the civilising influence of the Greek city-states that sport in the more modern, recognisable sense developed.

b) Greek city-states

This was the era of the ancient Olympic games, the religious festival of Zeus, the king of the Greek gods, which honoured him through athletic competition. Athletes from all city-states of ancient Greece were allowed to attend the games at Olympia, from the year 776 BC.

Through the sixth to the fourth centuries BC, there was a clearly defined class structure that was further reflected in the sports of most of the city-states. In Sparta, there existed the citizen body, which was given vigorous military and physical training, men and women alike, and the Helots, the conquered natives. Because of their rigorous training, the citizens of Sparta became the leading athletes in the ancient world, recording fully half of all victories at the Olympic games between 776 and 600 BC. However, because their training was purely for military purposes, they lost athletic refinement, and were quickly overtaken by the other states.

In Athens, it is probable that only the upper classes were allowed to compete in the Olympics. Training would last for 10 months, so only the rich could afford to be away from work for this length of time. Further down the social scale, gymnastics was more popular, and athletic events only became common after the introduction of subsidising and rewarding athletes.

This period in history was particularly violent, as the city-states were constantly at war with each other in order to attempt to conquer their neighbours and expand their empires. However, during the time of the Olympics, such was their importance, a truce would be called to all wars. The ethos of sport was to discourage violence, to reward physical prowess and to abide by strict rules. This contradicted much of Greek societal values, but was soon to change as the Roman Empire took over the Mediterranean region.

c) The Roman Empire

In the aftermath of the Greek empires, the Romans swept through much of the Mediterranean basin, and had conquered the majority of Europe by the first century AD. Initially the Romans were impressed with the Greek approach to sport, but unfortunately, in their attempts to copy their neighbours, Rome invariably increased the violence of pastimes. There are many possible reasons for this, one of them being the large amount of leisure time available to the Romans. Some suggestions are that there were 200 public holidays of which 175 involved 'games' or 'spectacles'. Roman society could function in this way due to their reliance on slaves. Over the years, people began to demand more and more spectacular performances, and this inevitably led to a rise in violence, including gladiatorial fights to the death, and the torturing and killing of humans and animals in the theatres. Thus, because of the extreme amount of leisure time citizens in Rome had, they needed exciting pastimes to overcome the boredom many may have felt. But these leisure forms were also used as a form of social control, so that their rulers kept the people, whose empire was built on violent conquest and slavery, quiet and happy.

Table 3   Sport in Britain: end of Roman Empire to 1880

500 AD	**Middle Ages** Local games played by peasants – very disorganised tournaments and jousts for nobility Catholic Church generally endorsed physical pastimes
1300 AD	Wars caused withdrawal of government and church support for leisure and sport – emphasis on military training
1400 AD	**Renaissance** Scholar–athlete became ideal for short period
1500 AD	**Reformation** Puritanism led to anti-sport and leisure policies – much greater effect on peasants than upper classes
1800 AD	**Industrial Revolution** Early pastimes limited by space and time for sport and leisure Work given highest priority – seen as a virtue 'Play' seen as sinful
1880 AD	**Age of modern sports** Expansion of middle classes – sport linked to character: 'healthy body, healthy mind' ethos Sports clubs established

The spread of the Roman Empire also meant that their leisure and sporting pastimes spread, and these of course then came to Britain. Small-scale amphitheatres were built, but mostly the Greek sports that the Romans had attempted to emulate were not adopted in Britain. When the Romans left Britain in the fourth century AD, their sports declined, and the Dark Ages and Middle Ages developed their own versions of sports (see Table 3).

d) The Dark and Middle Ages

Immediately after the fall of Rome, there was instability and chaos throughout Britain (fifth century AD). There was another regression in the civilising process, as people became more intent on survival, and so had less opportunity for other pastimes. As Roman society collapsed, Christianity began to take hold, and Roman ideas were shunned by the Church. By the eleventh century, the feudal system, with associated sports and games according to class, was beginning to develop. Farmers and serfs found few chances for sport and games, but did participate in simple dancing, running, catching and jumping games. Occasional mob football games, often played between two villages with few rules and no boundaries, emerged, usually on holidays such as May Day. The clergy discouraged such sports, but encouraged the more non-violent sports, while themselves taking part in hunting. They also advocated the 'glorification of body', supporting the nobility in their quest for a fit population, ready to fight at any moment. The nobility in turn had far more leisure time in which to pursue mainly military pastimes, such as jousting, and hunting. These more violent pastimes were discouraged for peasants, as it might give them the ideas and skills to mount a revolt. Overall, this period was marked by a decline in the complexity and variety of physical pursuits compared to the Greeks and Romans.

e) The Renaissance and Reformation

Both these periods contrasted greatly in the dominant societal approach to sport and leisure. The Renaissance, or 'rebirth' of learning, occurred after the sacking of Constantinople by the Turks in 1453. Scholars escaped to continental Europe from Britain, and revived Greek and Roman cultures. Sport therefore became a thing of interest, and served a purpose once more. One particular idea that gripped Europe was that of the 'universal man': the all-rounder who is intelligent, cultured, literate and also physically impressive. Books on the subject of physical education were published, most notably *The Courtier* in 1528, a book extolling the virtues of non-military-based sport for the first time. The Renaissance hit England by the end of the fifteenth century, and although peasant sport remained relatively unchanged, noble 'civilian' sport was now emphasised amongst the Tudor monarchs as being more important than military sports. The Tudor court therefore became a cultural and sporting model for society.

However, much of this changed during the Reformation. Calvinism and Puritanism began to take over the traditional religion of Europe, as there was a general feeling of corruption and over-indulgence within the Catholic church. The Puritans wanted to see a return to the purity of religious experience, a return to the authority of the Bible, and intense moral cleansing of society. Sport and leisure were seen as synonymous with sin, idleness and pleasure-seeking, and so were to be shunned at all costs. Work was regarded as the moral duty, and play a spiritual weakening.

Of course, these ideas took much greater hold of the peasants initially, but during and after the Civil War (1642–1649) decrees were made outlawing festivities and games. The main idea was that physical enjoyment could be equated to carnal enjoyment. Also, Puritan views were permeated with a concern for moral order in society – therefore, anything that tended towards disorder was banned. As most peasant sports lacked rules or refinement, they were inevitably the victims of this thinking.

f) The Industrial Revolution

In the interim period between the Reformation and the Industrial Revolution, little changed in terms of people's attitudes to sport. Play was still seen as a sin, and work a virtue, and these values very much helped the new industrialists to develop a disciplined, dedicated workforce. However, it was during this period that Thomas Arnold, the headmaster of Rugby School (1828–1842), began to introduce a new brand of Christianity into his school. The idea was that he would train pupils to become 'Christian gentlemen', sensitive to the problems caused by industrialisation and 'embourgeoisement' (the growing power of the bourgeoisie, the industrial middle classes who were gaining power and influence through the Industrial Revolution). He encouraged sport to be a part of the students' education, which was a new concept, in order to encourage team building and paternalism towards the lower classes. This also appealed particularly to the new industrial bourgeoisie, who could now afford to send their sons to public school. By the 1880s, most public schools had organised, compulsory sports as part of their life.

However, this was taken to extremes by groups such as the 'Muscular Christians' of the 1850s, who saw sport in schools as a necessary way of preparing young gentlemen for leadership while imbuing them with patriotic and Christian virtues. They also paved the way for much of the imperialism of the Victorian era (see Figure 4). Sport became a powerful tool in empire building: a civilising agent and a unifying force among the diverse cultures of the world. Furthermore, during the Crimean War (1853–1855) it was noted that

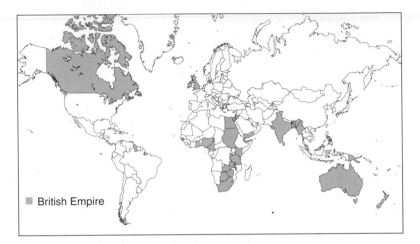

Figure 4 The extent of the British Empire at about 1900.

the majority of soldiers were unfit and in poor health. This, of course, led to a concern that military power, and ultimately control of colonies, would be lost.

Thus, the Victorians, on the back of a preoccupation with health, hygiene and morality created through rational recreation, provided swimming baths, parks, libraries and museums. So leisure, as well as sport, was promoted to develop a healthy military.

Therefore, many of the patterns of world sporting participation can be linked to the imperial Victorian era, and can help to explain why some sports developed in certain areas, and others did not (see Figure 4). This will be covered in more detail later in the book. Also, the Victorians left a legacy of leisure facilities, many of which are still in use today, and many of their ideals permeated into the early twentieth century.

4 Sport and Leisure in the UK in the Twentieth and Twenty-first Centuries

Since the turn of the twentieth century, sport and leisure have changed and developed dramatically in terms of time, money and participation. However, sport in particular has not changed a great deal, in that most sports played today were already in a recognisable form in the 1900s. It is best to look in more detail at sport and leisure now in terms of the *providers* of opportunities, as these very often dictate how we participate in sport or leisure activities.

a) Public sector provision

State provision, from both local and central government, has changed enormously since Victorian times. The emphasis and aims of government often dictated the way in which sport and leisure opportunities were provided:

- 1880–1900. State support, especially for voluntary efforts, to promote 'improving' leisure forms. Anything to benefit the Empire, in terms of fitness and 'civilisation', was encouraged.
- 1900–1939. Increased recognition of leisure as a legitimate concern of government in its own right – perhaps as a vote-winner?
- Once again, during the First World War, health and fitness of population were found wanting.
- 1944–1976. Leisure added to welfare: 'one of the community's everyday needs'
  - central government gives greater control to local authorities, but provision is 'permissive' rather than 'mandatory' (i.e. not required to provide facilities)
  - there is a major shift in leisure patterns, with growth of personal mobility (cars and motorways), leisure time and disposable income
  - leisure centres developed: 1960–1990 a total of 1200 built.
- 1976–1990s. Marketisation of service provision; leisure used as a tool for economies rather than social regeneration; residual provision with leisure as social policy tool in the inner city.
- 2000. Sport and leisure used more and more as political tools, with the emphasis shifting back towards excellence, and the hosting of major events.

Today, the structure of sport provision and participation in the UK works through a number of different levels within the public sector framework. Figure 5 shows the pattern of provision and legislative structure, and Figure 6 gives two possible models of sports participation, developed by the Sports Council to help explain patterns of sports participation.

Overall, public sector provision of sport and leisure facilities is highly important, but extremely expensive. Local authorities are reckoned to be spending approximately £1.14 billion every year. Most leisure centres run at a loss, as public leisure is heavily subsidised. The government attempted to introduce compulsory competitive tendering (CCT) in the Local Government Act of 1988, but this proved to be a failure. It was designed to:

"... improve efficiency by introducing the drawing up of a specification exposing outdated and restrictive practices and pointing out opportunities to deliver better services at a lower cost."

(HM Treasury 1988)

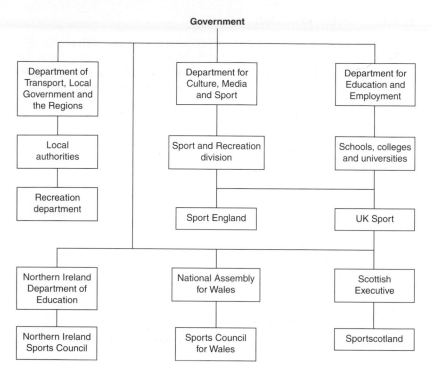

Figure 5 Organisation of sport in the UK.

Private companies were asked to bid for the right to run leisure centres, but then found that, without charging exorbitant rates, they could not run at a profit, and so most reverted back to local authority control.

b) Private sector provision

The private sector has now become the most important provider, in particular in terms of leisure. Companies saw that, with an increase in leisure time and disposable income, individuals would demand leisure services to fill that time, and would be prepared to pay to improve their leisure experience. Thus, leisure in particular has changed from a collective and egalitarian right, where the government provided facilities for all, to an individual, economically linked right, based around the consumer's ability to pay. Leisure is one of the largest and fastest growing industries, both in terms of its market share, and the number of workers.

Table 4 shows the numbers and percentage of the workforce in the leisure industry in the UK, and Table 5 shows how ownership of certain leisure products has changed over the last 30 years.

Model 1

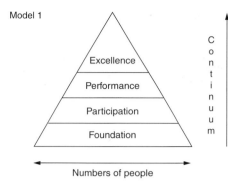

C
o
n
t
i
n
u
u
m

This particular model is rather limiting, as it assumes individuals must go through each level, which is not necessarily the case.

Numbers of people

Model 2

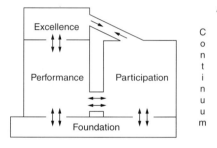

C
o
n
t
i
n
u
u
m

This model is perhaps more accurate, as it assumes that individuals can skip certain levels, or even regress in terms of their ability or participation,

Figure 6 Models of sports development.

Table 4 Numbers (in thousands) and percentage of workforce employed in leisure industries: 1930–1997

	Catering, pubs, hotels, restaurants, clubs, etc.	Entertainment, sports and recreation	Percentage in leisure
1930	351,000	78,000	3.5
1939	507,000	157,000	4.4
1950	629,000	212,000	3.9
1960	562,000	220,000	5.4
1970	568,000	242,000	6.5
1980	922,000	299,000	5.6
1990	1,219,000	469,000	7.6
1997	1,285,000	515,000	8.0

Table 5 Percentage of households containing leisure equipment: 1973–1997

	1973	1980	1983	1987	1990	1993	1997
Satellite dish	–	–	–	–	–	–	22
Home PC	–	–	–	25	28	31	34
CD player	–	–	–	–	24	45	67
VCR	–	–	23	56	75	82	89
Phone	48	75	79	85	88	91	95
Car	61	67	66	69	74	75	78

Source: General Household Survey.

These tables give details of both leisure outside the home and home-based leisure. Both have clearly gone through several years of growth, but at different rates and to different extents. In Table 5, for example, the rate of growth of home computers may seem remarkably slow. However, the 1985 figure of 25% refers to many machines that were far less powerful than the basic personal computer, and many of these households will have since upgraded their machines.

c) Voluntary sector provision

This is one of the largest and most diverse sectors of provision, as it includes all forms of sporting and leisure clubs and societies, such as scouts, choirs, amateur dramatics and some sports clubs. The idea is that for a nominal fee, people can participate in some form of leisure activity that is of interest to them, meet like-minded people and generally enjoy themselves in a social atmosphere. Often, the fee charged covers facility bookings, newsletters and membership fees. However, since 1995, National Lottery funding has also become available, so that groups can bid for money to develop their facilities.

SUMMARY

- Sport and recreation are closely linked concepts that are inevitably part of an individual's leisure time, unless they are a professional sportsperson.
- Definitions of sport, leisure and recreation vary dramatically, depending on your perspective.
- Sport and leisure can be traced back to their origins in the ancient world of the Mediterranean, and can be seen to have spread from there, through Europe, and into the modern world.
- Sport and leisure in the UK is provided by the public, private and voluntary sectors.

- Leisure has moved from being a collective and egalitarian right, to an individual, economically linked right, based around the consumer's ability to pay.

Questions

1. Using a similar continuum to that shown in Figure 1, draw up a diagram to represent three contrasting recreation/sporting pastimes.
2. For a sport or leisure activity you participate or are interested in, attempt to draw an organisational diagram, similar to Figure 5, to show how it is structured in the UK.
3. Using Tables 4 and 5, construct two graphs to represent the data diagrammatically, and attempt to account for the patterns shown on your graphs.
4. How are public, private and voluntary sectors of leisure provision interdependent of each other, and how has the emphasis on each changed over the past 100 years?
5. With reference to one urban and one rural area you have studied in the UK, compare the importance of each sector of provision in terms of facilities and opportunities provided in those areas.

2 Spatial Aspects of Sport and Leisure: Polarisation vs Dispersal

KEY WORDS

Economic factors: factors related to money, capital or investment that can also be attributed to the level of development of a country or region which may influence the location of sport or leisure activities
Environmental factors: characteristics of the environment that may influence the location of sport or leisure activities
Physical factors: closely linked to environmental factors, but concentrated more on landscape features than the overall environment
Political factors: characteristics of the government of an area, whether current or historic, which may influence the location of sport or leisure activities
Socio-cultural factors: factors related to society and culture, often as traditions, that may influence the location of sport or leisure activities
Technological factors: closely linked to economic factors, where locations may have technological experience, or lack of it, including infrastructure, communications and the capabilities to provide facilities

Similar to many geographical phenomena, sport and leisure have their own distinct patterns of distribution. So far this book has investigated the way in which sport and leisure has developed and spread over time through Europe, and therefore concentrated on sport and leisure in a small geographical area. In this chapter, the aim is to look more at the global pattern, and determine why specific sport and leisure activities occur where they do. The overall spread is an uneven one, showing distinct patterns of concentration and dispersal. The reasons for these are varied, and will be discussed in detail, with a case study provided for each example.

1 Factors Affecting the Distribution of Sport and Leisure

There would appear to be several major factors that affect the distribution of sport and leisure activities in general, although very often it is a combination of these factors that can affect sports. Conversely, several of these factors can also contribute to sports *not* developing in an area.

a) Physical/environmental factors

Physical and environmental factors generally include the natural characteristics of an area, and can have a major effect on the adoption or development of a sport. Such characteristics, and examples of sports and areas, can be seen in Table 6. For each of these factors, it is quite easy to see why a sport or leisure activity may take place in these areas. For example, competitive skiing requires snow, although as a leisure activity, dry-ski slopes have now been developed. Yet in both conditions, a slope of some sort is needed, so for skiing both climate and relief are important. Countries such as France and Canada, with adequate physical and climatic conditions, regularly dominate winter sporting events, whereas The Netherlands, for example, with no mountains and little snow, does not excel at these events (except skating).

Table 6 Examples of physical factors affecting sports and leisure activities

Physical factors	Sample environments	Associated sporting/ leisure activities
Climate	Cold conditions: snow, ice	Skiing, skating, tobogganing
	Coastal: wind, sun	Sunbathing, surfing, sailing
Relief	Mountain areas	Rock climbing, running, skiing, mountain biking
	Rolling hills	Hiking, horse riding
Proximity to water	Coastal	Sailing, swimming, scuba diving
	Lakes	Sailing, water-skiing
	Rivers	Canoeing, walking
Areas of natural beauty	National parks	Sightseeing, hiking
	World heritage sites	Sightseeing
	Coral reefs	Scuba diving

CASE STUDY: SCUBA DIVING

Scuba diving is one of the most popular leisure activities found around the coastal areas of the world. It, of course, requires a certain depth of water, so can also be participated in around lakes, reservoirs, quarries and rivers. However, the most common factor that attracts divers, apart from the water, are coral reefs. These beautiful, fragile ecosystems are under immense pressure from a variety of sources, not least the attentions of divers, and often, as in so many leisure activities involving natural wonders, the divers may well damage or destroy the very thing that they have come to see. Hands and fins can damage coral, and many will want to take away 'trophies' by which to remember their dive. These impacts will be covered in more detail in Chapter 5.

The distribution of coral reefs around the world (Figure 7) indicates that they are found, in general, between the tropics.

They are, of course, marine features, and the most popular are those close to land, such as the Great Barrier Reef off the north-east coast of Australia, or those of coral atolls rising from the sea bed, such as the islands of the Maldives, in the Indian Ocean. There are many other coral 'hotspots' (Figure 8), and these are in general the most popular places for divers, due to the beauty, challenge or ease of access of the reefs.

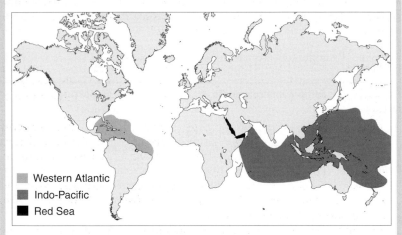

Figure 7   General global coral regions.

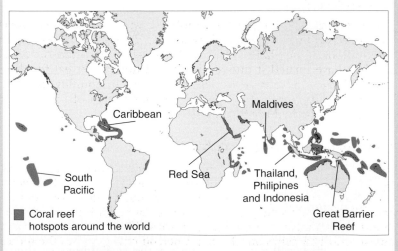

Figure 8   Coral reef 'hotspots' around the world.

Scuba diving in the Maldives

The Maldives in the Indian Ocean are a group of islands formed by volcanoes on the sea bed reaching almost to the surface. Coral reefs then grow on the rims of these volcanoes, creating the rings of islands, or atolls, which now form a haven for honeymooners and holidaymakers, and in particular for those interested in scuba diving. Crystal clear waters, shallow lagoons, diverse sea-life and spectacular coral features have all combined to attract investment and development in major resorts on the islands. These purely physical factors have made the Maldives one of the most popular dive sites in the world for divers of all abilities and experience, with an estimated 60% of all visitors participating. In several hard-core divers' resorts, such as Kuredu Island, 90% of holidaymakers will dive. There are hundreds of dive sites around the islands, with their own unique attractions, including:

- *Reefs*: the main dives along the edges of atolls that surround the lagoons and islands. Inner reef dives will be easier, in shallow, sheltered water, whereas those on the outer edges will be subject to surf and strong currents.
- *Kandus*: channels between islands or reefs, making them suitable for drift dives. As they are also deep areas where plankton thrive, they can attract large animals such as whale sharks, which in themselves are an attraction for divers.
- *Thillas*: a coral formation rising steeply, like a pinnacle from the atoll bed. They are a shelter for small fish, and therefore also attract larger fish seeking food.
- *Wrecks*: wrecks are relatively rare around the Maldives, but some that are accessible to divers have developed unique corals and associated ecosystems.

The leisure experience is also combined with surface water sports, sunbathing and fishing, again all related to the natural environmental conditions of the islands. Overall, the physical characteristics of the Maldives have turned it into a leisure and holiday retreat for those seeking beauty, adventure or just peace and tranquillity. In 1998, 396,000 tourists (more than the 300,000 population of the 26 atolls put together!) visited the 87 resorts (Lyon, 2000).

b) Economic/technological factors

Economic factors are those, unsurprisingly, concerned with the money involved in leisure pastimes or sporting activity. This could mean both from the point of view of the country itself, or from the view of individual participants. This particular factor is one that covers almost all participants in the modern world. The ability to participate almost invariably relies on whether a person or region has the money to be able to afford equipment or facilities. To this end, there can be seen to be a great disparity between more economically developed countries (MEDCs) and less economically developed countries (LEDCs) in terms of both facilities available, and, linked to that, the participation rates of various sports and leisure activities.

Technology is, of course, closely linked to the level of economic development of a country, and very often sport and leisure pastimes requiring a certain level of technological advancement will also therefore show a distinct pattern of global distribution. In this section, two particular issues are covered. First, the global distribution of tennis, a sport requiring defined space, specific equipment and one often associated with a certain level of affluence, is considered. Second, the effect of the level of technological development on leisure pastimes in an LEDC, Nigeria, is also studied.

CASE STUDY: SPORT AND ECONOMIC DEVELOPMENT – THE DISTRIBUTION OF TENNIS

The modern game of tennis as we know it is an adaptation and democratisation of the French game of 'royal' or 'real' tennis. An Englishman, Major Walter Wingfield, transformed the game by patenting equipment and publishing a set of rules in 1873. Tennis then spread rapidly throughout Europe, usually via British tourists. Standeven and De Knop (1998) tell us:

> "The spread and popularising of tennis owed much to the enthusiasm, status, and affluence of its devotees. Lawns on which to play, sufficient disposable income to purchase equipment and the 'right' social connections were all important. In the early days, even more than today, private incomes were essential."

This quotation gives the impression that in its infancy, tennis was only played by those who could afford the time and the equipment, a point reinforced by Bale (1982), who indicates that it was designed with the suburban middle-class in mind, where "… the possibilities of the suburban lawn were clearly recognised". To some extent the same is still true of tennis today. In the UK, Bale (1982) indicated that tennis clubs are found in a majority in the southern counties. Five of the top six counties (Greater London, Surrey, Kent, Essex and Gloucestershire) are associated with affluence, and it is noticeable that many of the counties with a dearth of clubs are the traditional, heavy-industrial areas with a greater working-class population.

Globally, tennis is not evenly spread either. Most successful tennis nations are drawn from the ranks of MEDCs, as shown in Table 7 (see page 23). This perhaps indicates that both money and leisure time are required to be able to participate.

Table 7   Origin of the top 100 male tennis players compared to gross domestic product (GDP) for 2003

Country	Population (millions)	GDP per capita (US$)	Players	Continent	Type
Spain	40	18,000	14	Europe	MEDC
USA	278	36,200	10	North America	MEDC
France	60	24,400	9	Europe	MEDC
Argentina	37	12,900	8	South America	LEDC
Australia	19	23,200	6	Australasia	MEDC
Germany	83	23,400	6	Europe	MEDC
Belgium	10	25,300	5	Europe	MEDC
Sweden	9	22,200	5	Europe	MEDC
Netherlands	16	24,400	4	Europe	MEDC
Russia	145	7,700	4	Europe/ Asia	LEDC (FCC)
Italy	58	22,100	3	Europe	MEDC
Brazil	174	6,500	2	South America	LEDC
China	1273	3,600	2	Asia	LEDC (FCC)
Croatia	4	5,800	2	Europe	LEDC
Czech Republic	10	12,900	2	Europe	LEDC (FCC)
Denmark	5	25,500	2	Europe	MEDC
Great Britain	60	22,800	2	Europe	MEDC
Morocco	31	3,500	2	Africa	LEDC
Romania	22	5,900	2	Europe	LEDC (FCC)
Switzerland	7	28,600	2	Europe	MEDC
Armenia	3	3,000	1	Asia	LEDC (FCC)
Belarus	10	7,500	1	Europe	LEDC (FCC)
Ecuador	13	2,900	1	South America	LEDC
Paraguay	6	4,800	1	South America	LEDC
South Africa	44	8,500	1	Africa	LEDC
Slovakia	5	10,200	1	Europe	LEDC (FCC)
Zimbabwe	11	2,500	1	Africa	LEDC
Canada	32	24,800	0	North America	MEDC
India	1030	2,200	0	Asia	LEDC
Indonesia	228	2,900	0	Asia	LEDC
Japan	127	24,900	0	Asia	MEDC

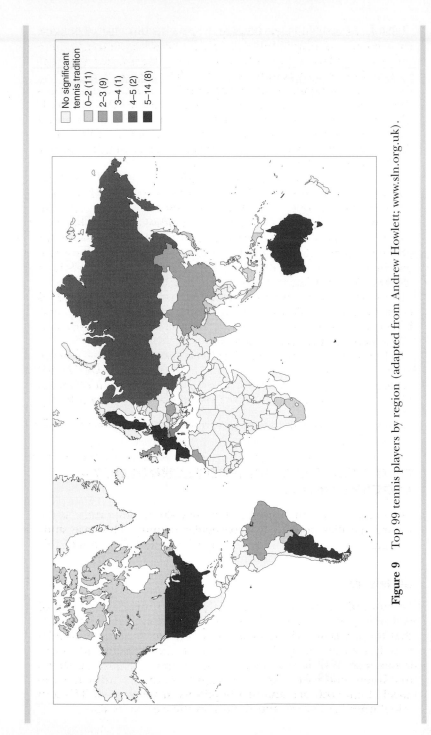

Figure 9 Top 99 tennis players by region (adapted from Andrew Howlett; www.sln.org.uk).

Table 7 shows the top 100 players from around the world, and their country of origin. Interestingly, and against the trend, there are a few LEDCs represented, including Argentina and many former Communist countries (FCCs). The former may well be due to the influence of the large number of British ex-patriots that settled in Argentina, and the latter due to the emphasis placed on international sporting success by the Central Committee of the Communist Party during the Cold War. This factor will be addressed later in this chapter, studying the former USSR and its satellites as sporting 'hotspots'.

The map in Figure 9 on page 24 shows that there is a definite clustering of talent in certain areas of the world – in particular Western Europe and North America – not surprisingly, the richest and most economically developed regions globally. The overwhelming supremacy of European and North American tennis players (70 out of 99) indicates that the need for equipment, courts and associated facilities can only be adequately provided in MEDCs. Yet, what is interesting is the lack of players in very economically rich countries such as Japan and Canada. This could be due to cultural reasons (no tradition of racket sports) in the case of Japan, or climatic or political reasons (lack of investment) in the case of Canada.

Thus, not only at the social level, but also when it comes to the elite nature of the sport, economic factors may well be of paramount importance in explaining the distribution of tennis players not only within a country, but also around the world.

CASE STUDY: LEISURE AND TECHNOLOGY – LEDCS VS MEDCS

Economic and technological factors may also be important in the leisure activities popular in a particular country. This case study compares the situations in the UK, an MEDC, and Nigeria, a LEDC.

UK leisure

Much of the leisure time in the UK is spent using some form of technology, often of a fairly complex electronic nature. The fact that the UK is an MEDC means that, on the whole, the population has access to a wider range of technologically advanced goods from a variety of sources. For example, Figure 10 shows that household leisure goods of high technology, and hence relatively high cost, are almost ubiquitous in the case of TVs and telephones, and are at almost 90% in the case of VCRs.

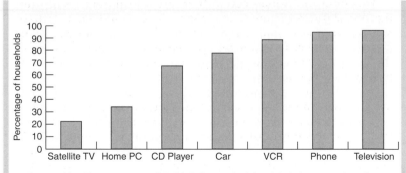

Figure 10 Percentage of British households with leisure technology in 1997. *Source:* General Household Survey.

Although some leisure time is also spent in more active pastimes, such as sport, or passive pastimes requiring little or no technology, such as reading, the fact that these goods are easily available to most households is significant. Thus, economics not only allows a greater level of technology to affect leisure time, but also allows for a greater choice in how to spend that leisure time.

Despite the figures, these are, of course, not the only pastimes available. Many others require few or no resources, such as walking or reading. The main feature is that economic and technological advancement increase the choice available to people. The case of Nigeria shows the converse – that choice can be severely limited by lower economic and technological advancement.

Nigerian leisure

If leisure in the UK can be said to revolve in a major part around technology, then the opposite can be seen to be true in LEDCs such as Nigeria. Leisure is still an important part of everyday life for some, but the leisure experience may well be very different.

A study by Ekpo (1991) of three tribes in Nigeria found that leisure pastimes varied greatly according to social class. Members of the upper class minority would participate in gambling, polo and golf, and the membership of sports clubs. Middle class pastimes would include indoor and table games, some sport and spectating. Among the lower classes, leisure was desired, but few had the opportunity. Those that did, participated in simple traditional games of running, throwing and catching, dance and activities with religious significance. In very few instances were technology or money a factor.

Wealthier individuals could therefore afford luxuries of prestige and status, and had the disposable income to be able to have significant leisure time. Their basic needs of food, water, shelter and income were met, freeing up time and resources for leisure, the enjoyment of comforts and greater convenience, in addition to being able to improve their economic situation.

Thus, this comparison, while only touching the surface, does indicate that the level of technological advancement can have a significant impact upon the leisure experience within a country. In essence, this means that the more disposable income available to individuals, the greater the opportunity for leisure participation. However, the difference occurs in the number of those able to pay for their leisure. In the more industrially and commercially advanced cultures of MEDCs, a much greater proportion of the population can afford leisure, and are prepared to spend on technology to improve their experiences. In LEDCs, the pattern is reversed.

c) Socio-cultural and political factors

In many cases, the traditions and culture of a society influence the pattern of sport and leisure activities more than anything else. This can be seen particularly in the case of Kenya, and their dominance of the sport of long-distance running. Many people would suggest that it is the physical landscape that drives their success, but, by the same token, why don't other mountainous countries such as Nepal, India and Peru excel at this particular sport? These factors will be assessed in detail in the case study for this section.

Political influences stretch back to colonial times, and in particular, the influence of the British Empire. The political decisions made during that time shaped much of the pattern of global sporting participation seen today. Sport is also seen to be of international significance to most countries, and many policies exist throughout the world to improve or focus on sport. The former Soviet Union is a prime example of where sport was seen as a weapon for politics during the Cold War, to the extent that the USSR became a sporting 'hotspot', excelling in most athletic events.

CASE STUDY: KENYAN RUNNING

It is a well-known fact that over the past 40 years, Kenya has produced some of the most talented distance runners, and in great numbers. This fact has been studied by many academics, keen to try and make sense of why so many great athletes come from just one LEDC in East Africa.

In fact, the production of these athletes is not geographically uniform over the country, but is concentrated in certain areas, where the tradition of running is the strongest. Figure 11 shows that the majority of athletes originate from the Rift Valley region of the country. More specifically, the Kalenjin tribe have been noted to account for the majority of medal successes over the years, as shown by Table 8. This shows their success, not only internationally, but also above their own countrymen.

This may at first glance seem to suggest that it is the altitude of 2000–3000 metres above sea-level that has allowed so many athletes to come from this region. There is evidence that leading a vigorous outdoor life in the thin air at such altitudes can help create the high aerobic capacity needed to succeed in distance running. However, there are several other tribes living at altitude in Kenya who have no tradition of producing runners, and as mentioned before, many other high-altitude countries produce

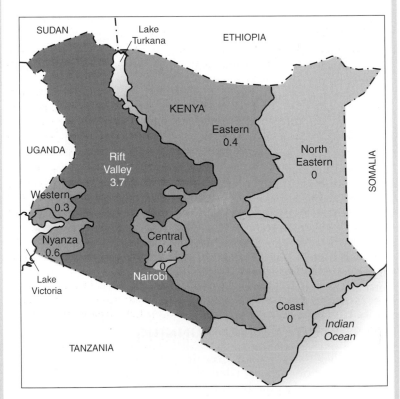

Figure 11   Per capita 'production' of superior Kenyan runners at the provincial level, Kenya, 1991 (after Bale and Sang, 1996).

Table 8   Olympic games medals (1964–1996) men's track
events 800–10,000 m

	All medals	Gold
Kalenjin	26	8
USA	10	3
Great Britain	8	1
Non-Kalenjin Kenya	7	4
Morocco	7	3
Germany (East and West)	6	1
Ethiopia	5	1
Finland	4	3
New Zealand	4	2
Tunisia	4	1

Excluding boycotted games of 1976 and 1980.
Adapted from Manners (www2.umist.ac.uk/sport/2_art2.htm).

few or no runners. Despite this, running camps are still held at altitude to train athletes, but simply because of the benefits of this to the elite athlete. It requires more than just living at this altitude to produce the numbers that have come out of Kenya, and the Kalenjin tribe in particular.

The focus of this section is the socio-cultural impact on running, and it is here that Kenya finds its reason for success. Poverty is a key factor, as many Kenyans are very poor, and see running as a way of escaping from the everyday grind. But also, running is part of their cultural heritage. Rural children may run between 5 and 10 kilometres to school everyday, and sometimes home for lunch as well! The warrior tradition of the Kalenjin means they are conditioned to resist pain, and endure hardship all through childhood. This prepares them mentally as well as physically for the pressures of long-distance running.

Overall, there are several factors that combine to allow Kenyans to be so successful in long-distance running. But ultimately it is their traditional way of life, and the culture of running ingrained into their way of life that is the dominant factor. The case of the physical environment here is merely coincidental, but, of course, training at altitude also hones the edge they already hold due to their culture.

CASE STUDY: THE BRITISH EMPIRE – POLITICS AND THE SPREAD OF SPORT

The British Empire, as described in Chapter 1 and shown in Figure 7, has been identified in many sources as being a key factor in the distribution of sport seen around the world today. The influence of the colonists was often very wide ranging, and the peculiarly British sport of cricket is specifically identified here. However, it is also necessary to study why certain countries, even though part of the Empire, may *not* have taken up these sports.

The spread of cricket

The modern game of cricket has undergone many changes over the years, but the current incarnation sees the game being played all over the world. In areas that traditionally have not accepted the game, such as Japan, the USA and the Middle East, the vast majority of the players tend to be ex-patriots from test-playing nations (countries that have adopted the game, and play to the highest standard internationally).

Figure 12 shows where these test-playing nations can be found, and it can be seen that the countries identified were all members of the British Empire. What is also noticeable is the way in which these nations are all either close to the equator, or in the southern hemisphere. The reasons for this are unclear, and will not be assessed in detail here. Suffice to say, cricket has been widely accepted in these countries, and they were all members of the British Empire. Thus, political factors may be identified as being the deciding factor for the adoption of cricket as a national sport.

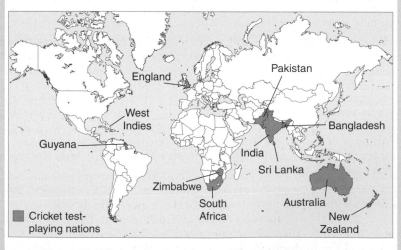

Figure 12   Global distribution of cricket test-playing nations.

2 A Comparison of the Colonial Influence in Australia and the USA

The British Empire left behind its mark in terms of sporting traditions on many countries, but, in some places, the traditions were changed, improved or even not adopted in a serious way. Australia and the USA tell two very different stories of the effect of colonialism on the development of sports.

a) Australia

In 1788, Australia was first used as a penal colony for the Empire. Criminals were transported there as punishment for crimes committed. However, transportation eventually was abolished in 1840, and free settlements began to spring up around the country, particularly around the coastal regions. By 1891, it had become the most urbanised country in the world, with cities focused around coasts. After the transport of criminals was stopped, a powerful middle class of pioneers, with enough money to gain passage and then to set up their own businesses, settled in the country. It was these settlers that had a distinct desire for their own national identity, and no longer wished to be a branch of the British Empire.

Certain sports, like swimming, developed naturally, with many beaches, a good climate and a cleanliness ethic transferred from Britain. These would almost certainly have developed without colonial influences. However, cricket, the ultimate colonial game, became extremely popular. Many Australians realised that the country could not compete financially with Britain and the rest of the Empire, but could try to out-perform them at their own game. And so grew the desire to beat the 'old enemy'.

Football, on the other hand, never took off in Australia. It has always been associated with industrialisation, as seen in the north of England during the Industrial Revolution. Middle class pastimes tended to dominate, as there was only a small industrial working class in Australia. All of its technology was inherited, and much of its wealth derived initially from primary industry. As a result, rugby, being a predominantly middle class game in Britain, became immensely popular, in both its Union and League forms. Again, Australia saw this as another opportunity to humiliate their old masters in the international arena. And so a brand of political warfare, based around sporting success, came in to being. Australians saw the sportsfield as the best, and at the time only, place where they could compete with Britain.

Yet, they did not turn entirely to British sports. They also developed their own sport of 'Aussie rules' football, a hybrid version of rugby and Gaelic football, for a sense of national pride. Possibly, they saw this as a way to underline and promote their national identity –

trying to beat Britain at their own games, while also playing their own, Australian sports as a symbol of their independence.

b) The USA

During the 1700s, the eastern seaboard of the United States was settled by Europeans, who came to fight over the rich, previously untapped natural resources to be found there. European culture took over, and colonial sports developed. However, the development was not uniform, as the initial settlements were introverted and suspicious of the colonies of other countries. They therefore developed sports specific to their culture. In the English colonies, this meant that cricket and hunting became popular, as pastimes of the upper classes who were generally the founders of colonies.

However, the War of Independence in 1775–1783 saw a shift in the types of sport participated in. 'Frontier sport' took over, as exploration of the fledgling United States required specific skills to be honed, and so shooting, fishing and survival pastimes became more popular. Team sports were less emphasised, as the ethos of survival was very much to depend on oneself. In the hostile frontier wilderness, you could not necessarily count on the support of others.

From 1861 to 1865, the Civil War took place, and the USA moved further from English pastimes. Rugby, which was popular in universities at the time due to the influence of the privileged middle class, began to develop into American football as colonial influences decreased. Other quintessential American sports such as baseball – a development of the English games of rounders and cricket – also began to increase in popularity. The overall pattern was therefore one of a desire to move away from colonial influences. This indicated to the UK and Europe in general that the USA was free from their former colonial masters, and were prepared to establish their own national identity, partly through sport, and a rejection of common European pastimes. Football, rugby and cricket all declined in popularity as the new country threw off all previous colonial influences.

This attitude is, of course, very different to the way the Australian nation felt. Where the USA rejected their colonial background, to the point of discontinuing participation of popular pastimes, Australia embraced it in order to compete with their former colonial masters. They wanted to prove to them that their freedom and national identity was a source of pride, and that they could beat them at the very sports they invented, and brought to their colonies.

3 Sport and Leisure 'Hotspots'

The term hotspot is one that suggests an area of sporting or leisure activity well above average for the world as a whole. Many hotspots are

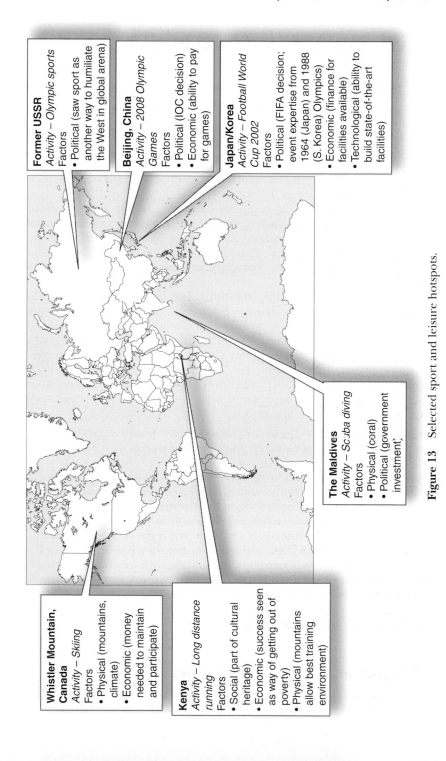

Former USSR
Activity – Olympic sports
Factors
• Political (saw sport as another way to humiliate the West in global arena)

Beijing, China
Activity – 2008 Olympic Games
Factors
• Political (IOC decision)
• Economic (ability to pay for games)

Japan/Korea
Activity – Football World Cup 2002
Factors
• Political (FIFA decision; event expertise from 1964 (Japan) and 1988 (S. Korea) Olympics)
• Economic (finance for facilities available)
• Technological (ability to build state-of-the-art facilities)

The Maldives
Activity – Scuba diving
Factors
• Physical (coral)
• Political (government investment)

Whistler Mountain, Canada
Activity – Skiing
Factors
• Physical (mountains, climate)
• Economic (money needed to maintain and participate)

Kenya
Activity – Long distance running
Factors
• Social (part of cultural heritage)
• Economic (success seen as way of getting out of poverty)
• Physical (mountains allow best training environment)

Figure 13   Selected sport and leisure hotspots.

identifiable as being areas that attract a great deal of attention for a specific reason. For example, the term has already been used in this chapter to identify areas of coral reef that are considered to be the most important for serious divers (see Figure 8). Most of these hotspots will therefore be linked in to the factors identified in the previous section, and very often will be due to the right conditions in a number of different areas. Figure 13 shows the links between various sport and leisure hotspots, explaining briefly why these areas can be considered as such.

All of the areas indicated in Figure 13 are known in some way for their degree of sporting excellence or leisure appeal, and so could perhaps be considered as 'hotspots'.

However, some are known more for the **talent** they produce (Kenya, former USSR), whereas others can be considered **locational** hotspots because they attract large numbers of people for a specific reason (Whistler, Maldives). This chapter has covered in some detail both **talent and location hotspots**, in the detailed Kenyan and Maldive case studies.

This distinction in itself is interesting, but even more interesting is the decision of a body, for example FIFA (Fédération Internationale de Football Association) or the IOC (International Olympic Committee), to artificially create a hotspot by awarding places major sporting events. From the examples, Japan/Korea (2002 World Cup) are areas that would not initially have been considered traditional hotspots in the sense of football, as they have little history of success in the game. Other factors must therefore be deemed to be important in creating such hotspots.

CASE STUDY: BEIJING 2008 OLYMPICS

The awarding of the Olympic games to a country is one of the highest sporting honours and, as such, ensures that the city in which the games take place wins enormous international recognition, in the form of becoming a locational 'hotspot'. This case study assesses the various factors that are important in the creation of an Olympic city, and while Beijing itself is the focus of this study, it will also attempt to explain the reasons behind cities *not* being selected to host the games, and so not becoming Olympic hotspots.

The bid for the 2008 games

Originally, 10 cities bid for the 2008 games, with another three cities intending to bid, but eventually pulling out. The decision was eventually given to Beijing, and the reasons behind this need to be assessed. However, it is also interesting to assess the reasons why the other cities were *not* awarded the games (Table 9).

Table 9 Cities bidding for or showing interest in the 2008 Olympic games

City	Country and status	Comments
Beijing	China – Communist	Eventual winners of the bid
Toronto	Canada – MEDC	Runners-up to Beijing, with a strong, all-round bid including a detailed environmental policy
Paris	France – MEDC	Experience of 1998 World Cup a factor but, being in Europe, is too soon after Athens 2004. Also spread of venues and pollution were problems
Istanbul	Turkey – MEDC	Games have never been in Turkey, but they may have problems coping, particularly with weak infrastructure
Osaka	Japan – MEDC	Well supported by their government, but too soon after Nagano Winter Olympics, as well as being far from North American time zone
Bangkok	Thailand – LEDC	Although they recently hosted the Asian Games, there were problems over construction and finance
Cairo	Egypt – LEDC	Very little known about how the city intended to approach their bid, but it is thought poor infrastructure would have been a limiting factor
Havana	Cuba – LEDC	Again, little known about the bid, but political factors may have been an issue
Kuala Lumpar	Malaysia – LEDC	After hosting the 1998 Commonwealth Games, the city has facilities, but bid hastened through. They may bid again for 2012 or 2016
Seville	Spain – MEDC	Fell short in 2004. However, have good support, so may well bid again in the near future
Buenos Aries	Argentina – LEDC	Did not bid, but could accommodate North American time zone. Plenty of bid experience over the years
Rio de Janeiro	Brazil – LEDC	Did not bid, but could accommodate North American time zone
Monterrey	Mexico – LEDC	Did not bid. Although Mexico staged the games in 1968, Monterrey has no previous bid experience

Based on the information presented at http://www.gamesbids.com

The first five cities in the table are the candidate cities, or the ones that the IOC voted for as the strongest bids. The next five entered the bidding, but were eliminated in the first round as their bids were not considered to be strong enough to continue. The final three entertained the idea of bids, but in the end decided not to bid. What is particularly noticeable, however, is the fact that seven of these eight cities are in what have traditionally been considered to be LEDCs, and four of the five candidate cities MEDCs, with China being somewhere in between as a transition economy. Perhaps this has some bearing on the final outcome. What is obvious is that the Olympics require extremely advanced facilities and infrastructure, possibly beyond the budgets of most LEDCs. China might be the exception here, and was chosen because of the centralised nature of the economy, and the organisation that such a Communist country may be able to muster.

Beijing's bid

Beijing had bid for the Olympics 8 years previously, and was beaten into second place by Sydney, by only two votes. This time around, they were the clear winners, as Table 10 shows.

Beijing already had experience of staging a major athletic event. In 1990, the 11th Asian Games were held there, which allowed for the construction of several facilities. These included the International Convention Centre, hotels and museums as well as the National Olympic Sports Centre and the Asian Games Village. The Olympic Green is backed up by the venues and related facilities used during the Asian Games, an easy transport network, a populated area, and an array of commercial and cultural facilities (see Figure 14). Ten years after the Asian Games, this area has already been developed into one of the most attractive places in Beijing.

Table 10   Voting for 2008 Olympic games
candidate cities

	First round votes (%)	Second round votes (%)
Beijing	44	56
Toronto	20	22
Paris	17	18
Istanbul	14	9
Osaka	6	–

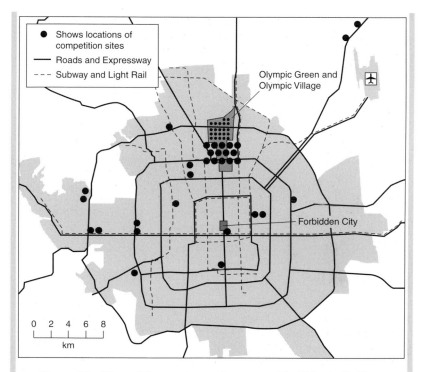

Figure 14   Plan of the current and proposed facilities in Beijing.

One other major contentious issue was China's human rights record. However, whereas in 1993 Beijing had brushed aside questions about human rights, and arguably lost out because of it, here they were far more open, and used the games in a more politically astute way, claiming that the development and capital would allow for a rethink of policies, and, as a result, further impressed the judges. Although among many charities, non-governmental organisations (NGOs) and governments there is still caution and bitterness over the decision, Beijing seems to have the expertise, technology, facilities and backing to be able to organise the games effectively. What will be under scrutiny is the behaviour of the Chinese government before, during and after the games. Despite this, they are set to become a locational 'hotspot' as a result of the 2008 Olympics.

SUMMARY

- Sport and leisure activities vary spatially across the world for a number of different reasons: environmental, physical, socio-cultural, economic, political and technological.
- Sport and leisure also differ between MEDCs and LEDCs, often as a result of the above factors.
- Very often, a combination of factors is important in the explanation, rather than just one, and the explanation of why an activity develops in an area is very complex.
- Sport and leisure 'hotspots' can develop due to the talent found within a country, so they become known for a particular sport, or due to the development of specialist facilities that attract participants.

Questions

1. Draw up a table of the six important locational factors for sport and leisure developments detailed in this chapter, and attempt to come up with examples for each, both in positive and negative terms.
2. Identify the reasons why **two** contrasting sports develop in different areas, and in different ways.
3. Choose **two** contrasting leisure activities in your local area, and attempt to account for the reasons why they have developed in the way they have.
4. 'The British Empire is more responsible than any other single agent in the spread of sport around the world'. Discuss.
5. Summarise the arguments for and against the Chinese bid for the 2008 Olympics to be held in Beijing. Use the six locational factors to help you.

3 The Impact of Sport and Leisure on Communities

The impacts of sport and leisure can be assessed in many different ways, and from a variety of angles. The next three chapters will look at the ways in which sport and leisure impacts on communities including both people and the places in which they live, economies and the environment, both natural and built. In particular, issues of sustainability must be focused on, as these become increasingly important in the setting up and running of major developments or activities of any type in the world today.

In this chapter, the emphasis will be on how sport and leisure have both positive and negative impacts on communities, in terms of the people and on the places in which they live. There is, of course, some overlap here with the environmental chapter (Chapter 5) in terms of the built environment, but this chapter will attempt to assess it from the community aspect, rather than the urban region in general.

1 The Impact of Sport on Communities

The impact of sport and leisure on people can be divided simply into positive and negative, particularly when considering the development of facilities. One of the most common ways of studying the impacts of sports or leisure developments on communities is by looking at **externalities**. Essentially, an externality is the unintended impact of a development or event on the surrounding area, which will theoretically decrease with distance from the development or event. Because the externalities may reach out in all directions, they create what is known as an externality field (see Figure 15). However, not surprisingly, as distance from the centre decreases, then theoretically so should the externalities, in a process known as **distance decay**. This distance decay creates what is known as an **externality gradient**.

Figure 15 shows how, in theory, a stadium at point *S* creates externalities, which are felt over varying distances:

- *S–X*: radius where negative externalities dominate, and so impact adversely on the population.
- *S–N*: radius where negative externalities can only be found, but also positive externalities can be found. Outside of this, externalities will only be positives.
- *S–P*: area outside of which no externalities will be felt.

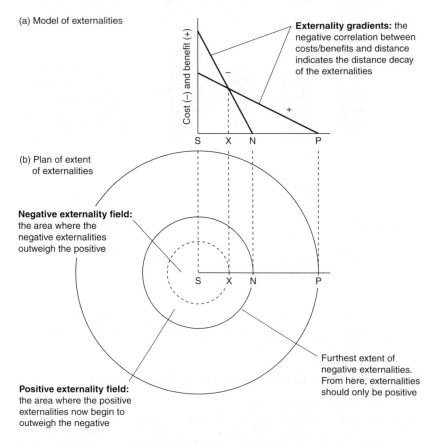

(a) Model of externalities

Cost (−) and benefit (+)

Externality gradients: the negative correlation between costs/benefits and distance indicates the distance decay of the externalities

−

+

S   X   N   P

(b) Plan of extent of externalities

Negative externality field: the area where the negative externalities outweigh the positive

S   X   N   P

Furthest extent of negative externalities. From here, externalities should only be positive

Positive externality field: the area where the positive externalities now begin to outweigh the negative

Figure 15 Theoretical model of externality fields, gradients and distance decay (after Bale, 2000).

a) Externalities and sport: the case of football

Applying this theory to reality has been performed on many occasions, and in particular there are several studies on the externalities created by football stadia on the communities around them. Bale (1990) studied in great detail the externalities of football stadia, both positive and negative, and the perceptions of those who lived both nearby, and further afield from, such developments. Figure 16 represents the contrasting opinions and perceptions of those living near football stadia, and the general public, and Table 11 shows some of the typical externalities associated with football stadia.

These charts show that the perceived negative externalities as described in Table 11 are perhaps not as bad as most people would believe. Serious nuisance seems to be a lot less prevalent than outsiders would think, and that, in fact, most people who live close to such developments may well get used to their presence. The sense of pride and identity that one perhaps could gain from living close to a stadium may well help to counteract the negative externalities.

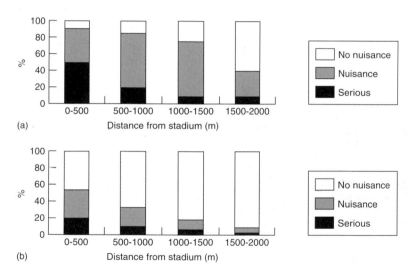

Figure 16   Percentage of general public who (a) felt proximity to stadium may cause nuisance and (b) perceived actual nuisance. (Based on Bale, 1990.)

b) Example: the externalities of Arsenal football club

In recent years, Arsenal has caused some controversy in the locality with plans to build a new, state-of-the-art stadium at Ashburton Grove, near to the current area of Highbury, north London, which is an area in some need of redevelopment. Much of the planning for this has been in full view of the local community, and so there have been

Table 11 Some externalities occurring due to football stadia

Positive		Negative	
Externality	Description	Externality	Description
Increased revenue	On match days, shopkeepers and pub landlords in the locality of the stadium can expect to increase takings	Noise	With the increase in the number of people within a neighbourhood, and the match itself, comes the noise of the crowd
Sense of identity	The stadium may be a source of pride to the local population, and as a result enhance people's view of the area	Congestion	An increase in traffic close to the stadium, and in surrounding roads, could cause traffic jams on match days
		Hooliganism	The real fear of many local residents, although today one that tends to be less of an actual, and more of a perceived, threat

many arguments put forward, both for and against the development. The club itself has highlighted the many positive externalities it has created in partnership with the local community, including:

- after-school football and hockey clubs for boys and girls
- short-mat bowls for senior citizens
- trainee programmes in leisure management and coaching for 30 young people per year
- free football, cricket, hockey and mini-tennis lessons for 12 local primary schools
- the Arsenal charitable trust, distributing £50,000 per year to local good causes.

(This information is taken from the club's own website.)

The club, in providing all these facilities and services for the local community, has clearly thought that it has built up considerable goodwill, and so has proposed a new stadium development that will, according to them, benefit the community greatly:

- £5 million upgrade to Holloway Road underground station
- new improved pedestrian facilities and controlled parking zones to be developed
- 2300 new, affordable, houses to be built as part of the complex
- 1900 new jobs to be created

(again, taken from the club's website).

Yet despite all these seemingly good points, local residents are clearly worried about the new stadium. In January 2000, the Islington Stadium Communities Alliance (ISCA) was formed in order to oppose the proposed stadium development, believing that a new development of the size expected would be inappropriate in a densely populated and congested area. The contentions from the ISCA are that:

- the 60,000-seat, 15-acre development will impose too many demands on already overloaded public services and transport
- more traffic and pollution will be created
- several conservation areas in the vicinity will have to be removed
- a proposal for over 40 events each year is too many
- Islington's largest industrial estate will be demolished, eradicating over 60 local businesses, although many are due to be rebuilt at the nearby Lough Road site.

Of course, it is not yet possible to fully predict the outcome of the development when it goes ahead. Suffice to say, the club already produces a wide range of externalities, some good and some bad, within the local community, and the new, larger development will only increase these. Local residents are worried that the negative externalities will be the ones with the major impact.

This is not the only relocation and redevelopment of a football stadium. Southampton (detailed in Witherick and Warn, 2003), Oxford, Portsmouth (detailed in Bale, 2000) and Wimbledon, to name but a few, have all moved to new sites (although the latter admittedly moved to the already built National Hockey Stadium in Milton Keynes), and Liverpool are looking at the possibilities at the moment. All eyes will be on the impacts created by such a high-profile move, and whether or not such a development can be sustainable within the local community. Likewise, the development of the new national football stadium is sure to create its own high-profile externalities.

c) Sporting externalities in LEDCs

Sporting impacts vary greatly, depending on the activity and the facilities required, and these are quite often separate from those externalities associated with large-scale developments. Sport can have positive influences in terms of social gains and behavioural adjustment. For example, in the UK, during the 1960s the development of leisure centres as a national phenomenon was seen as a way of combating teenage delinquency. Sport is still promoted as a way of bettering oneself, and getting out of inner-city cycles of crime and poverty.

In many LEDCs, sport plays a similar role in the community, and is seen as a way of improving the quality of life for many living in poverty. As has already been suggested in the previous chapter, sport in the form of running has been seen as a way out of poverty for many Kenyans. Even for those who do not escape poverty via this route, it is still a major part of the Kenyan way of life in rural areas and the Rift Valley.

The most positive influence of sports programmes in LEDCs may be those associated with young people, especially those in low-income households with little access to education. They are being used as a way to keep children in school, provide education about drug and alcohol abuse, educate them about health, the environment, and, in particular, about sexually transmitted diseases such as AIDS. One key example of this, assessed in more depth in Chapter 7, are the United Nations Environment Programme (UNEP) 'Nature and Sport Training Camps', launched in Nairobi in 2001, which teach children the importance of looking after the environment through sports participation and coaching.

However, sporting externalities on communities have not been so positive when related to larger-scale developments. Many LEDCs have large sports facilities, paid for by borrowing huge sums of money from the World Bank or other investors, which have been used for a variety of purposes. But have they been useful additions for the local community?

- *World Cup: Mexico 1986.* Mexico gained the honour of hosting the soccer world cup from Columbia, which failed to meet the deadline for provision of facilities and infrastructure. Poor and hungry inhabitants of the major city venues were dismayed, and demonstrated at the thought that money was being directed towards football, and that many of them were living in poverty. As was written as graffiti on the side of one stadium: "*No queremos goles, queremos frijoles*", meaning "We do not want goals, we want beans".
- *Central American and Caribbean Games: San Salvador 2002.* Waste from spectators and competitors alike built to 4500 tons as the organisers of the games refused to take responsibility for its management. They simply did not have the funds to be able to cope with that amount of rubbish, which led to associated pollution and, consequently, health problems.
- *Olympic Games: Beijing 2008.* Although perhaps no longer classed as an LEDC, China's plans have certainly impacted on the community. Tramps and beggars were cleared off the streets, traffic was

halted all across the city and brown winter grass was painted green to enable the visiting IOC dignitaries to see Beijing in all its glory, however false that image may have been.

These are just three examples of how sports events have created negative externalities on communities in LEDCs. There are undoubtedly many more instances of sporting externalities both in LEDCs and MEDCs, but very often the research into these focuses on the economic impacts, rather than the social. This particular aspect will be assessed in much more detail in Chapter 4.

2 The Impact of Leisure on Communities

The impact of leisure upon communities can be seen in a similar light to the impacts of sport. Externalities from leisure developments, and leisure participation or consumption, can be felt in the local community in much the same way as those felt from stadia. But the range of developments is often much greater. For example, leisure developments can include anything from cinemas and shopping centres to parks and other open spaces. This section will focus on the externalities of entertainment facilities in particular, such as pubs and cinema complexes, before considering further ways in which leisure pursuits can have an impact on communities.

a) The case of leisure in cities

In theory, the development of leisure facilities in an area should improve the quality of life for people living in that region due to the redevelopment of run-down areas, and the creation of new, exciting facilities. In the following examples, one focuses on leisure redevelopment in a formerly derelict waterway area, and the second gives details of a specific type of development:

- *Birmingham*: the redevelopment of the canal system in the early 1990s (detailed fully in Prosser, 2000) led to extensive leisure facilities. These include the International Convention Centre (ICC), the National Indoor Arena (NIA) and Brindley Place, all connected by walkways and canal-side paths. The development was originally intended to be a cultural one, attracting international musicians and entertainers, but as the success of the project spread, so did the appeal of the area. Soon, bars, restaurants and shops all lined the waterways, and, whilst it brought in money, local people complained about the fact that money was being spent on leisure for the wealthier sectors of the population. Also, the huge increase in bars and night clubs on Broad Street, adjacent to Brindley Place and the ICC, meant that large numbers of party-goers made the area noisy, and less attractive through loutish behaviour. Yet, leisure developments have continued, and the entire city centre including the infamous Bull Ring Centre has been levelled to make way for new leisure facilities, in a £450 million scheme. This has now reopened as a huge shopping development, to include a vast, modern Selfridges department store. Not only that, but the huge central Royal Mail sorting office has now been redeveloped into the Mailbox, an entertainment centre geared around bars, restaurants and expensive designer shops.

• *Superpub developments in the UK:* during the 1990s, many breweries such as Bass and Whitbreads saw the opportunity to develop a new form of entertainment centre. There were growing numbers of student and young, single people in major cities around the country, most of which had a reasonable disposable income. The breweries saw these people as the ideal target for 'superpubs', large, often themed pubs where sporting events could be watched, and the drinks were cheaper than in many other establishments around the area. Although seemingly a good economic idea, creating jobs and attracting people into the city, the knock-on effect in terms of litter, traffic congestion, fumes, noise and disturbance generated by the increased numbers have all had adverse effects on the local communities where these developments have been set up (Jones and Hillier, 1997). Such developments include the growth of Wetherspoons and Yates' Wine Lodges, for example.

Other cities have seen their waterways as particularly good areas to redevelop: London (Docklands), Newcastle (Quayside) Swansea and Gloucester (both docks) have all undergone redevelopment for the purposes of leisure. These developments impact on the built environment as well as communities, and this will be assessed in more detail in Chapter 5. As for the 'superpubs', despite the complaints often received by local authorities, the development of these looks set to continue, as economic positive externalities are thought to outweigh social negative externalities.

b) The case of leisure in rural areas

Leisure can also have major impacts on rural communities, but in many different ways to urban areas. The impacts on rural areas in Britain are very much associated with the movement of people from urban areas to the countryside for leisure purposes. The impacts of countryside recreation and leisure such as hiking, cycling and camping are very often highlighted as being mostly environmental (see Chapter 5), but the following case study shows that leisure does have impacts upon communities in rural areas.

CASE STUDY: SECOND HOMES IN RURAL AREAS OF THE UK

For many years now, there has been growing concern in rural areas and the National Parks of England and Wales that too many houses are being purchased by urban dwellers to become second or holiday homes. The demand for such homes has risen drastically in recent years, and with this the sectors of employment within local communities have changed markedly. Figure 17 shows where the most popular second home areas are found, which often result in declining agricultural employment, and a growing leisure and tourist market. This has meant that traditional employment has declined, while tertiary sector jobs in areas such as bed and breakfast, outdoor pursuits and tea shops has increased dramatically.

However, leisure has further knock-on effects that are not immediately apparent. The Lake District and other National Parks, such as Exmoor, have suffered from a rise in house prices as the properties in the Parks are in high demand. In the Lake District alone, it is estimated that some 60% of houses are second homes, lived in only for a few weeks of the year. This means that not only is the population falling, but also that many people who work in Grasmere, for example, are forced to move away, outside the Park to towns such as Kendal, 32 km away. This then adds further impacts on the community in terms of traffic congestion, as

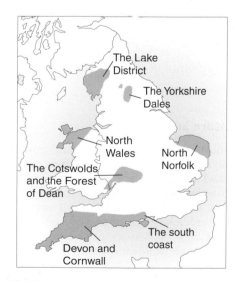

Figure 17 The main concentrations of second homes in England and Wales.

people have to commute in along narrow country lanes (Jones, 1998). Villages also lose their community feel, becoming 'ghost towns', populated very often for less than 2 months of the year. The story is very similar in Exmoor, but there they have tried to combat this by proposing to stop people from buying second homes. This scheme is unpopular because it may also have a negative effect on the area, as houses will initially remain too expensive for locals, and so the houses will be left unpurchased as well as unoccupied. The knock-on effect could also be a decline in local services as tax revenues decrease. Guidelines are still to be set up, but some restrictions seem inevitable. However, the government is considering raising Council Tax on second homes from 50% to 100%, as has already happened in South Hams in south Devon, although this is more likely just to provide an increase in tax revenue rather than to combat the effects of buying second homes.

Overall, the impact of leisure on countryside communities is perhaps not as immediately obvious as the externalities identified in the sport section, and leisure in urban areas. Much of the impact in rural areas tends to be environmental as much as anything, and this will therefore be followed up in much greater detail in Chapter 5. The social impacts are apparent in terms of the impacts on people's daily lives. The nature of sport and leisure means that very often community feeling is given less weight than the economic and environmental impacts they have. However, it is difficult to divorce them completely from each other – much that affects rural and urban communities can be seen as environmental, and many impacts are closely linked to the economic success or failure of a development.

SUMMARY

- The development of sporting facilities can have knock-on effects on local communities.
- The knock-on effects, known as externalities, can be both positive and negative, and are often unintended.
- Externalities theoretically decrease with distance from the development, with the positive effects being felt over a wider area.
- Leisure creates externality fields, particularly in cities, associated with facilities and areas for leisure pastimes.
- In the countryside, externalities on communities tend to be more focused, but no less prevalent.

Questions

1. Make a list of all the positive and negative externalities you can think of in relation to a specific sporting or leisure development. Rank the externalities in order of amount of impact, and justify the order you come up with.
2. For a stadium or other large-scale sporting development in your local area, attempt to identify and map the main externalities associated with it. You should consider the views of:
   a) local businesses
   b) local residents.
3. Discuss the impact of a leisure activity or facility that you have studied on its local community.
4. "The development of waterfront areas brings more problems than it solves". With reference to a city you have studied, assess the validity of this statement.

4 The Impact of Sport and Leisure on Economies

So far sport and leisure have been assessed in terms of their impact on communities, and in several places their impact on economies was also considered. This is because the impacts of sport and leisure are varied and inextricably linked. This chapter will attempt to study the impacts of sport and leisure on economies in more detail. This will include the way in which fundamental economics can be applied to sport and leisure, for example supply and demand and the multiplier effect. The way in which sport and leisure contributes to economies, and the use that governments in particular have made of sport and leisure in economic development, both on a local and national scale, will also be studied. Generally, sport and leisure are seen as being beneficial to economies, and are often used as a way to regenerate areas suffering economic recession. They can be seen to provide:

- revenue
- jobs
- opportunities for economic diversification
- multipliers in the wider local or regional economy.

1 The Economics of Sport and Leisure

In assessing sport and leisure's impact on economies it is necessary to introduce some key fundamental economic concepts that can be applied to them. We next consider two areas that can be applied. The examples and theory given refer first to leisure, and in the second instance to sport.

2 Demand and Supply Relationships

Demand and supply is one of the most fundamental of economic concepts, and will be applied here specifically to leisure. It can also be applied to sport in a similar way.

The relationship between demand and supply is extremely important in all forms of economics. In terms of leisure, demand can be seen as the measure of a consumer's use of a good or service. Supply is thus how much or how little of that good or service is available to the

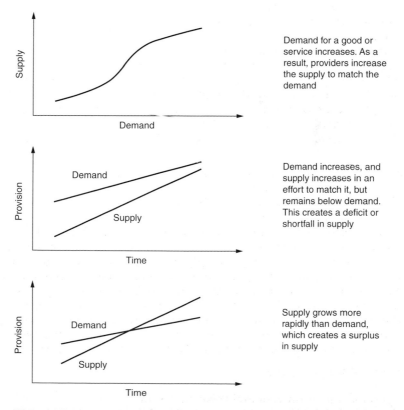

Demand for a good or service increases. As a result, providers increase the supply to match the demand

Demand increases, and supply increases in an effort to match it, but remains below demand. This creates a deficit or shortfall in supply

Supply grows more rapidly than demand, which creates a surplus in supply

Figure 18   Demand–supply relationship graphs (after Prosser, 2000).

consumer. The relationship between them determines the amount of money made or lost (i.e the economic impact), and helps plan for future trends. Figure 18 shows three simple graphs that represent the basic relationships between supply and demand.

The relationships between supply and demand exemplified here are, of course, theoretical, but can be applied to almost any situation involving leisure provision and use of leisure time. However, demand and supply change their characteristics over time. They can both increase or decrease independently, and it is these changes and their relationship that can influence the impact of leisure on the economy. The supply of leisure comes from three main sources: the public sector, private sector and voluntary sector. These providers are assessed in Chapter 1, and so will not be studied in detail here.

a) Types of demand

Demand, as stated above, does not remain constant, and can be split into three main areas:

- **Effective demand**: this is the demand for specific leisure goods or services from those who have actually participated in a leisure activity.
- **Potential demand**: this is the demand for a good or service that could occur, but has not yet, due to two main reasons:
  - *deferred demand*: potential participants are aware of an activity, but do not take the opportunity to do so, perhaps through lack of time, money, etc.
  - *latent demand*: participants are unaware of an activity, but would participate if they became aware.

These types of demand are heavily targeted by providers in order to increase effective demand.

- **Elasticity of demand**: the demand for a good or service is sensitive (or not) to changes in the price of that good or service, e.g. business air travel is inelastic, whereas holiday travel can be considered to be more elastic. Elasticity of demand in particular has a marked impact on economies.

These demand types can once again be applied to many scenarios, but perhaps more importantly for providers of leisure in attempting to predict the demand that will occur. This is known as **demand forecasting**, and is used so that over- or under-supply of a good or service does not occur.

b) Demand forecasting

Demand is a constantly changing variable, and as a result it is necessary for providers to attempt to forecast what the demand for a good

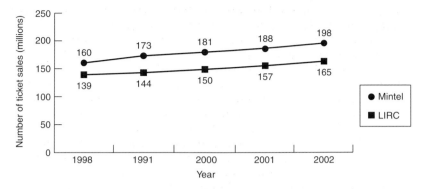

Figure 19 Predictions from two market research companies (adapted from Tribe, 2000).

or service will be, so that over- or under-provision does not occur. The most common way of predicting future demand is to use statistics of past and current trends in demand. This then allows:

- Planning for future development and production to occur.
- Planning for expansion of production base, and allows for staffing, etc., to be organised in advance.
- Earmarking of money in advance for particular functions, and being able to lobby for investment.

Forecasting is usually carried out by companies, using market research, employed by providers of leisure. Examples of such companies include the Leisure Industries Research Centre (LIRC) and Mintel. Forecasting can be a risky business, particularly if wider trends in consumer tastes and a limited range and history of data are used. Figure 19 shows the demand forecast, made in 1998, for cinema attendance from these two companies over a 5-year period.

Interestingly, the two lines are generally 20–30 million sales apart along the whole forecast, which suggests very different research techniques. Undoubtedly, current and past data on numbers will have been assessed, but, as it turned out, both predictions were relatively inaccurate. The actual figure for 2002 was in fact 176 million, 11 million greater than predicted by LIRC, and 22 million less than predicted by Mintel! This can therefore be seen to be something of a guessing game. Yet, if predicted correctly, in the case of cinemas, people will not have to be turned away from showings because of over-booking, and auditoriums will not be empty, causing the company to waste money, because of a lack of demand.

CASE STUDY: LEISURE DEMAND IN THE UK

The demand for leisure services and activities in the UK has in general increased over the past 40 years. This is due to two key trends:

- an increase in leisure time
- as Figure 20 shows, the amount of time we work during the day has, on average, decreased from 296 minutes in 1961, to 246 minutes in 1995. To account for this, domestic work time and overall leisure time have increased, but the emphasis on the activities taken part in has changed.

An increase in leisure time

The reasons for the reduction in working time are varied, but often focus around the improvement of communications tech-

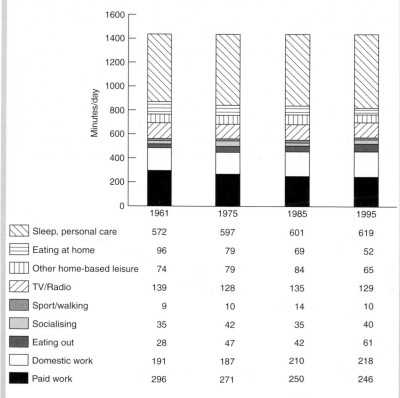

	1961	1975	1985	1995
Sleep, personal care	572	597	601	619
Eating at home	96	79	69	52
Other home-based leisure	74	79	84	65
TV/Radio	139	128	135	129
Sport/walking	9	10	14	10
Socialising	35	42	35	40
Eating out	28	47	42	61
Domestic work	191	187	210	218
Paid work	296	271	250	246

Figure 20 National Time Accounts/day: 1961–1995 (*source*: www.statistics.gov.uk).

nology, and the desire for a less stressful lifestyle. Thus, there is a trade-off between work and leisure: the longer a person works, the more precious each leisure hour becomes, until a point is reached where the benefit of the additional income gained from work is not worth the loss of leisure time incurred.

This means that leisure activities increase to fill the non-work time. Eating out in particular has increased in popularity, as has socialising overall. As a result, therefore, home-based leisure and TV watching have decreased. The reasons for this could be attributed to the second key trend.

An increase in disposable income

Disposable income is the amount of money a person or household has left over after spending money on the essentials, such as food, travel, bill payments and the like. Figure 21 shows the trend, in terms of an index, of household disposable income between 1971 and 2000.

This indicates that, over this period, the amount of disposable income available to households has more than doubled (the index meaning that the value of the disposable income, in 1970, was 100, and that in proportion this had risen to 210, or more than twice the 1970 value). Of course, inflation will have played a part in this, but overall households will have seen a rise in the amount of money that can be spent on luxuries, above and beyond the essentials. This is therefore also money that can be spent during the longer hours of leisure time experienced by the majority of the population. Overall, consumer expenditure and disposable income have increased by 2.5% per annum in real

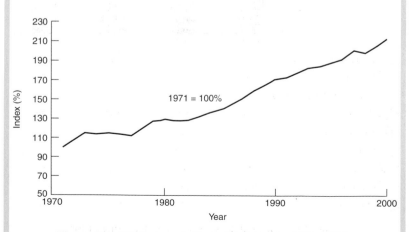

Figure 21   UK index of disposable income: 1971–2000.

terms over the past 25 years, and it has been projected by the government that this trend will continue.

Having established that leisure time and spending have increased, it is necessary to determine exactly what contribution leisure demand makes to the economy. According to the government, the leisure industry:

- is the fastest growing sector in the UK
- employs 2.5 million people, equating to one job in ten
- creates one in five of new jobs.

If the impact of sport on the economy is also included, figures from Sport England show that:

- for every £1 of government support received, sport gives back £5 into the economy
- sport tourism was estimated to be valued at £1.5 billion in 1995
- consumer spending on sport in 2000 was £15.2 billion
- sport provides 400,000 paid jobs, and 108,000 voluntary sector equivalents.

It can therefore be seen that both sport and leisure contribute a large amount to the UK economy as a whole. At a local level this varies, but, in general, the demand for leisure is increasing, and as a result, the supply and therefore the employment, provision of services and opportunities will rise to match it. If combined, the impact can be even greater. For example, it is estimated that five million people watched the 2003 Rugby World Cup Final between England and Australia in 10,000 pubs around Britain, drinking 37 million pints of beer and making a £20 million profit! (Born, 2003.)

3 The Multiplier Effect

The multiplier effect, or economic multiplier, is a tool for studying the wider economic impacts of a particular phenomenon. In terms of sporting events, which will be assessed here, the multiplier:

> "... converts the total amount of additional expenditure in the host city to a net amount of income retained ... after allowing for 'leakages' from the local economy."
>
> (Gratton and Taylor, 2000)

Essentially, the multiplier works out the amount of money that remains within an area, as a result of a number of different factors acting on the local economy. Figure 22 shows some of these factors. This model indicates that if enterprises have the commitment to their local area, and attempts to retain as much money in the area as

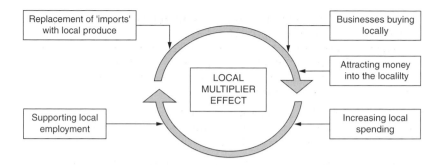

Figure 22   The local multiplier effect (after Westall *et al.*, 2001).

possible, then it will ultimately benefit in ways initially unconnected with the enterprises concerned. For example, further jobs may be created, and redevelopment within an area may attract further investment from outside.

This is also the idea behind a multiplier in relation to a major sporting development. However, when the private or public sector purchases goods or services from outside the host region or city, that money no longer contributes to the multiplier effect, and the associated benefits are lost to the host – this is referred to as leakage.

a) The proportional multiplier

The proportional multiplier is one of the simpler ways of measuring the impact on the economy of a major sporting event. This can be expressed by the formula

$$\frac{\text{direct} + \text{indirect} + \text{induced impacts}}{\text{initial visitor expenditure}}$$

where:

- initial visitor expenditure is the amount of money spent by visitors to an area
- direct impacts are incomes and jobs resulting from the initial expenditure in local businesses
- indirect impacts are incomes and jobs generated by businesses spending visitor expenditure to buy local goods and services
- induced impacts are the incomes and jobs resulting from spending income that is obtained as a result of visitor spending.

Although this is seen as a relatively simple mechanism in theory, the practice of actually obtaining all the relevant data is almost impossible, owing to the numbers of people and businesses involved.

Gratton and Taylor (2000) use Sheffield to exemplify the phenomenon, and borrow figures from other wider studies. The figure quoted is 0.2, which means approximately 20% of visitor expenditure remained in the city following the World Student Games in 1991. In the context of the next case study, the data to work out the proportional multiplier are not readily available, but the economic impacts of a large-scale sporting event, in this case the Manchester Commonwealth Games in 2002, can still be assessed.

CASE STUDY: IMPACT ON ECONOMIES OF LARGE-SCALE SPORTING EVENTS – 2002 COMMONWEALTH GAMES, MANCHESTER, ENGLAND

The staging of a major event is universally seen as a matter for national pride, due to the international exposure a country gets, and the chance it gets to 'sell' itself on a global stage. Equally, the local area will invariably feel a sense of pride and achievement, no matter what the outcome of the event.

Most recent studies of such events have highlighted the economic importance of large-scale events to countries and host cities alike:

- 1984 Los Angeles Olympics: made a profit of £215 million
- 1992 Barcelona Olympics: made a profit of approximately £1.5 million
- 1996 Atlanta Olympics: was expected to raise approximately £2.9 billion for the economy of the US state of Georgia.

But it is important to note that exceptions do occur. Whilst the political and global image rewards can be great, the financial burden can far exceed these:

- 1972 Munich Olympics: lost £178 million
- 1976 Montreal Olympics: lost £692 million.

In the UK, the economic importance of major sports events became apparent after Euro '96, when 280,000 overseas visitors spent £120 million. Despite the risks, in 1996 Manchester bid for and was awarded the Commonwealth Games in 2002. The city had been through several periods of growth, decline and redevelopment, and the Commonwealth Games was seen very much as a way to improve, in particular, east Manchester. This area had been the home of the traditional industries in the city: coal, textiles, chemicals, engineering and steel. However, it was severally affected by the economic recessions of the 1970s and 1980s, losing 60% of its employment between 1970 and 1985 (www.gameslegacy.com). As a result, the games were seen as a way in which to improve the economic situation, via the redevelopment of the area.

In terms of the economic benefits from the games, the statistics speak for themselves:

- an estimated £600 million worth of investments were secured
- around 6100 full-time jobs were created
- an estimated extra 300,000 people will visit the city, spending £12 million.

All of these figures are associated with the building of new sporting facilities, transport links and housing. Much of the economic success has also been attributed to the inclusive way in which the games-related activities were developed, and the fact that, when planning for the games, quality was always at the forefront of all policies.

There are few indicators of the proportional multiplier in Manchester, but it is likely to be relatively favourable, as it is a large city that can, if necessary, provide the majority of things required for the games developments. Relevant employment figures include:

- 2320 jobs in east Manchester
- 2400 jobs for the city of Manchester
- 1920 jobs for the north-west of England.

In terms of capital invested in the region:

- £277 million was spent on construction and regeneration
- transport schemes costing almost £800 million brought forward, with £125 million of public investment.

Finally, it is estimated that the Games will encourage 30 million people to consider Manchester as a business and visitor destination. The Manchester games have therefore very much been seen as a great success for the organisers, and although there will certainly have been leakages from the local economy, the economic benefits are undeniable.

SUMMARY

- Supply and demand relationships are central to the study of the economic impacts of sport and leisure.
- Demand occurs in various different forms, and can be assessed via effective, potential or elasticity of demand.
- Supply of a good or service depends on demand forecasting, so that providers will be able to estimate how much of a good or service must be available to consumers, so that there is neither a surplus nor a shortfall.
- Demand is very much affected by key variables such as available leisure time and disposable income, both of which have a bearing on how much and the type of leisure consumed.
- The multiplier directly takes into account the effects of sport on the local economy, and is a good indicator of how much impact an event can have on an area.
- Major sporting events are generally seen as being beneficial, not only to national pride, but also to the economy in the form of the multiplier effect.

Questions

1. Give examples that would fit each of the three supply–demand relationships identified in Figure 18.
2. Give examples of goods and services that are demand elastic and demand inelastic (e.g. those that react to changes in price, and those that do not)? Explain your answers.
3. For one major, large-scale, irregular sporting event that you have studied, discuss its economic impact on the local community and on the country as a whole.
4. Compare the impact of your chosen event to that of any major spectator event that is part of an annual domestic cycle, for example Wimbledon or the FA Cup Final.

5 The Impact of Sport and Leisure on the Environment

The environmental impacts of sport and leisure have become one of the most important areas of research in recent years, due to the current trend of sustainability studies, and there is a wealth of information available on a variety of different sports, leisure activities and environments. In this chapter, the aim is to concentrate on the positive and negative impacts on both built and natural environments, by concentrating on case studies for each.

In terms of the positive and negative aspects of sport and leisure, it is often considered that these activities can provide benefits to urban environments, but cause more problems in natural environments. The case studies will attempt to redress this, and give a balanced view of both. In the built environment, this will include the positive and negative aspects of sport and leisure developments. In natural environments, the management strategies used to rectify impacts, and even improve areas damaged by sport and leisure, will be assessed.

1 The Sustainability of Sport and Leisure Environments

The future of sport and leisure will be discussed in more detail in Chapter 7, but it would be useful now to take a moment to identify

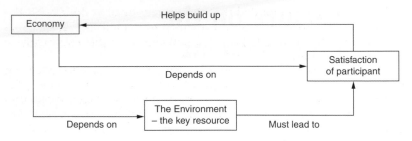

Figure 23   The importance of the environmental resource to
sport and leisure.

why the environment is an important consideration in any sport or
leisure scenario. Figure 23 suggests the idea that the integrity of an
environment, whether it be built or natural, is essential to an activity,
so that it can then benefit the area economically, and thus links back
to what was covered previously in Chapter 4.

Without a well-maintained or attractive environment, participants will
be less likely to want to spend their leisure time in the area, and so will
seek the experience elsewhere. As a result, there will be adverse effects
on the area's economy, as participants' capital is spent elsewhere.

Sport and leisure therefore depend to a great extent on the integrity of the environment in which they exist, while at the same time
they have a wide-ranging diversity of impacts on that very environment upon which they depend. This paradox can very often be hard
to reconcile, particularly in the case of the natural environment.
However, sport and leisure developments are very often seen as
beneficial to the urban environment.

2 The Impact of Sport and Leisure on the Built Environment

As has already been discussed in Chapter 3, the impact of major sporting developments on communities in urban areas can be both positive and negative, very often depending upon one's viewpoint. The
development of the new Arsenal Stadium at Ashburton Grove has
been seen to be very controversial, not least in the fact that the independent inspector's report stated that:

> "... proposed Compulsory Purchase Orders, which would allow
> the council to force local businesses off their sites so that the
> land would be cleared for the stadium project, should not be
> allowed because there was 'no compelling public interest' case
> for them."

> (Conn, 2003)

The report recommended that the project be abandoned, yet the Deputy Prime Minister, John Prescott, overruled the inspector's judgement. This meant the project could begin, despite expert advice that the area would not benefit.

Sport and leisure developments have often been used to redevelop areas within cities that have required regeneration. In Sydney, for example, many of the sites used for the Olympic Games' facilities were former industrial wastelands, heavily polluted brownfield sites that were given a full development programme. The success of the 2000 Olympic Games on the back of the facilities has benefited the area enormously, and so the impact on the environment in this case has been extremely positive. There are many cases of research into large-scale sporting developments and their impact on the built environment, as indicated in the references. Yet, large-scale leisure developments also have a very large part to play in urban regeneration, as in the case of Swansea in South Wales.

CASE STUDY: THE REDEVELOPMENT OF THE SWANSEA BAY REGION, SOUTH WALES

Swansea has been an area that has seen many changes over its history. After coal and iron ore were discovered in the region during the Industrial Revolution, Swansea became a centre of metallurgical expertise, with developments of new foundries and smelting sites after the building of the first dock in 1851, on the banks of the River Tawe.

After the prosperity of the late nineteenth and early twentieth centuries, Swansea's heavy industries began to decline through a series of economic depressions and competition from abroad. By the 1920s, most of the largest smelting works in the Lower Swansea Valley had closed, and the North Dock closed in 1928.

By the 1950s the Lower Swansea Valley was one of the largest areas of uninterrupted dereliction anywhere in Britain, and was also one of the most polluted urban areas, with the waste of 70 years of intense heavy industry dumped all along the banks of the River Tawe.

However, the Lower Swansea Valley and the city centre were regenerated over a 30-year period, beginning in the mid-1960s, via schemes to develop industry, retailing, leisure and tourism. Figure 24 shows the wider context of the Swansea Bay conurbation. The areas focused on in this case study will be those identified in Figures 25 and 26, which show schematics of the city centre and the Lower Swansea Valley, as well as the areas around the docks at the mouth of the River Tawe.

Figure 26 shows the location of a variety of different sport and leisure facilities built to regenerate the urban environment, as

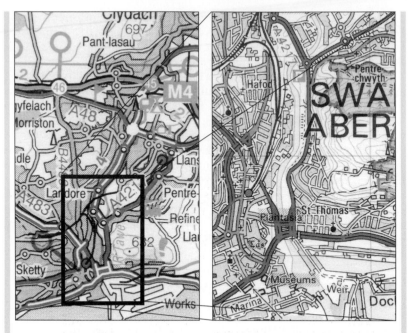

Figure 24   Map of the Swansea Bay area.

well as improve the social and economic fortunes of the city. The development was based around a seven-park scheme, reclaiming and improving former industrial areas and the declining city centre.

- *The Riverside Park*: as the name and photograph suggest, this is an area of reclaimed industrial land alongside the river. The area in the foreground is part of the former White Rock metal works. The area was heavily polluted before the clean-up efforts of the 1970s and 1980s.
- *The Quadrant Shopping Centre*: in the 1970s the shopping area of Swansea was extended southwards, and extensively redeveloped and pedestrianised to allow for a more attractive and improved shopping experience.
- *The South Dock*: once a thriving dock, this area has now been redeveloped for housing, leisure and tourism, to include bars, museums and the city marina.
- *Swansea Leisure Centre*: the focus of the South Dock development, this is one of the most popular and busiest of South Wales' leisure attractions
- *Castle Square*: since 1993, a strategy to upgrade the city centre has taken place, once again trying to improve the shopping environment. Here, Swansea Castle is also used as a tourist feature.

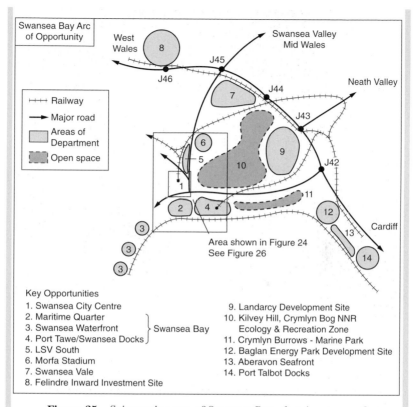

Figure 25 Schematic map of Swansea Bay, showing areas of development opportunity.

- *North Dock Retail Park*: in the 1980s the central business district (CBD) finally expanded eastward down on to the former North Dock site (renamed Parc Tawe) on which was built a ten-pin bowling alley, a ten-screen cinema, Plantasia and large retailing outlets.
- *Morfa Stadium*: this area, as part of Swansea's Leisure Park, was found among playing fields in the northern part of the Lower Swansea Valley. Although it was developed over 10 years ago, the go-ahead has been given to develop a new, 20,000-seater stadium and leisure complex, due for completion in 2005.

The combination of these developments has served to transform Swansea from a depressed, former heavy industrial city into a thriving leisure and tourist hotspot.

However, not all the redevelopments have successfully regenerated Swansea. The St David's Shopping Centre, next to the Quadrant, was developed along with the rest of the CBD, but

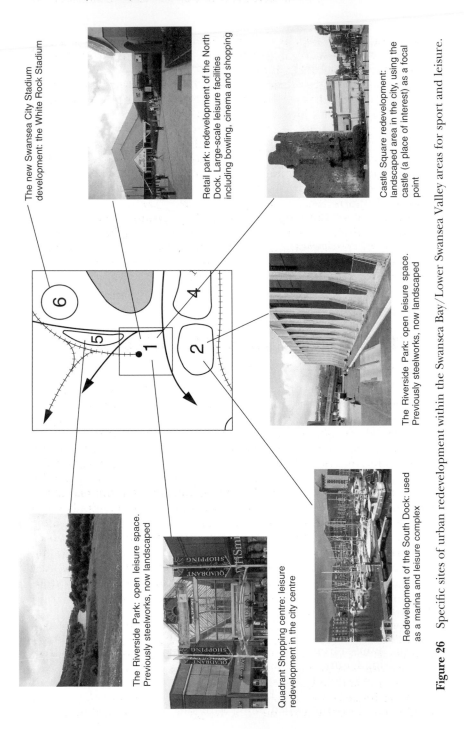

The new Swansea City Stadium development: the White Rock Stadium

Retail park: redevelopment of the North Dock. Large-scale leisure facilities including bowling, cinema and shopping

Castle Square redevelopment: landscaped area in the city, using the castle (a place of interest) as a focal point

The Riverside Park: open leisure space. Previously steelworks, now landscaped

The Riverside Park: open leisure space. Previously steelworks, now landscaped

Quadrant Shopping centre: leisure redevelopment in the city centre

Redevelopment of the South Dock: used as a marina and leisure complex

Figure 26 Specific sites of urban redevelopment within the Swansea Bay/Lower Swansea Valley areas for sport and leisure.

most shops have been forced to close due to lack of custom. The reason for this is the proximity of the larger, more varied shopping facilities available in the centre of the city.

Overall, though, the developments have appeared to be a success, and the urban environment has been much improved by the development of leisure facilities in particular.

There are numerous examples of redevelopment schemes in urban areas based around sport and leisure, and there is a wealth of literature on these. Newcastle, Bristol and Manchester have all undergone schemes based around leisure, and Southampton and Portsmouth have both undergone redevelopment based around sports developments. There are also some excellent examples from outside the UK, including Olympic cities such as Sydney, whose 'Green Olympics' in 2000 were hailed as a triumph of putting sustainability into practice, by recycling resources and using brownfield sites for developing many depressed and derelict areas of the city.

3 The Impact of Sport and Leisure on the Natural Environment

So far, this chapter has dealt with the impact of sport and leisure on the built environment, using Swansea as an example of how they can improve and enhance urban areas. Very often, the impacts of sport and leisure on natural environments are seen as detrimental, and careful management is needed to maintain the integrity of the environmental resource. This ties in with the ideas in Figure 23, where the quality of the resource is considered vital to the quality of the recreational experience of the participant. However, this may ultimately mean that parts of the natural environment are manipulated to be able to sustain the levels of use that they experience. In some cases, this means changing the environment entirely, with the creation of damaging facilities such as ski resorts and golf courses, and so the term 'natural environment' is no longer applicable. Thus, in this part of the chapter, the 'natural environment' can be equated to non-urban areas, because even the countryside as we know it in the UK is a largely human construct.

Sport and leisure activities are often cited as being some of the most detrimental to the natural environment, although there can be positive as well as negative impacts. These can be seen in Table 12, and are assessed in more detail in relation to specific activities and sensitive habitats and species in Table 13.

These impacts are of concern to certain groups of stakeholders within the natural environment, although their views will undoubt-

Table 12   Selected environmental impacts of sport and leisure

Positive impacts	Negative impacts
Increased opportunity for conservation	Pollution
Money from participants	Erosion
Increased protection for wildlife	Disturbance of wildlife
Becoming *part* of the experience	Physical damage
	Overcrowding/increase in traffic

edly conflict in many ways, depending on their viewpoint (see Figure 27), and it is often the actions of these interest groups that extend impacts, both positive and negative.

An assessment of the impacts of sport and leisure on the natural environment requires a study of a selection of issues from Tables 12 and 13 and Figure 27.

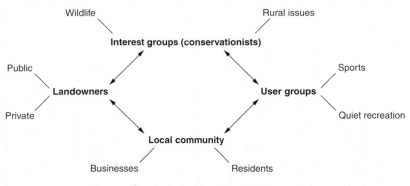

Figure 27   Stakeholders in the countryside.

While there are many sport forms in which people participate in the countryside, as shown in Table 13, it is perhaps skiing and golf that are the most popular, and therefore could be said to have the largest impact.

a) Skiing

Although skiing has become the most popular of mountain sports, it is extremely damaging to the environment. Because of its popularity, it has also become one of the most common economic activities in mountainous areas, and, while its financial rewards can be enormous, the demand worldwide has become unsustainable. It is estimated that there is a global market of 65–70 million people, of which 50 million use the

Table 13 Specific impacts of selected activities (adapted from House of Commons Environment Committee 1995)

Activity	Sensitive habitat/species	Potential impact
Aircraft (helicopters, microlights, light aircraft)	Nesting and non-breeding birds; Coastal – birds in breeding season	Disturbance to bird populations – abandonment of nesting sites; reduction in breeding time
Angling	Lakes and rivers – fish and invertebrates; breeding and non-breeding birds	Disturbance to birds; damage of bankside vegetation
Caving	Cave formations; bats	Disturbance of geological features
Climbing	Geological and geomorphological formations	Removal of vegetation; risk of rock falls
Golf	See the separate section in this chapter	
Mountain biking	Sensitive vegetation and soil types (especially when wet)	Localised damage; conflicts with other users
Off-road vehicles (4 × 4 cars and trail bikes)	Heathland, grassland; coastal – shingle; dunes; saltmarshes; beaches	Damage to vegetation; conflicts with other users; erosion of unconsolidated material
Orienteering	Woodland	Localised damage
Paintballing	Woodland	Trampling and erosion; vegetation loss; associated developments
Riding	Lowland heath, grassland; woodland	Trampling and erosion; vegetation loss
Skiing	See the separate section in this chapter	
Walking and dogs	Upland and lowland heath; grassland; montane heath; Coastal – sand dunes, beaches	Localised damage to vegetation and soil erosion on key routes; trampling on dunes, beach erosion; disturbance to breeding birds
Water sports	Lakes and inland waterways; birds; coastal regions	Disturbance to breeding and non-breeding birds; conflicts with other users; pollution; bank erosion

Alps annually. As a result, an infrastructure consisting of 40,000 ski runs and 14,000 ski lifts is capable of handling 1.5 million skiers per hour! (Ward cited in Standeven and De Knop, 1999.) Because of these numbers, resorts have become larger and therefore more damaging to the environment. Specific environmental impacts include:

- Clearing trees, rocks and flattening slopes weaken soil and increase avalanche risk.
- Many resorts rely on artificial snow, using vast quantities of water and electricity.
- Flattened areas give no chance for vegetation recovery in the summer.
- In the quest for new experience, off-piste skiing ventures into fragile, unprepared areas that have a carrying capacity too low to be able to sustain it.

However, it is the building of resorts in these fragile environments that has enabled skiing to take-off, and, as a result, has created more demand, which, while providing income, also has to be satisfied.

CASE STUDY: WINTER OLYMPICS – ALBERTVILLE, FRANCE, 1992

The Winter Olympics, in a similar way to the Summer Olympics, are seen as a great honour for the host country and region, and may help to regenerate the area economically. As a result of this, great efforts are put into winning the bid for these Olympics.

In the 1960s, the exploitation of the Alps had been a national policy in France, and huge resorts began to develop. Yet, often, little thought was given to their impacts – rubbish was left on the slopes, thousands of tons of waste were produced daily, sewage plants struggled to contain pollution and much irreparable damage occurred to Alpine slopes. Fewer tourists visited the region during the 1980s, and so it was felt that new development was needed to boost the area.

Albertville in the Savoie region was designed to be the attraction that brought people, and top-class skiing, back to the Alps. However, the inevitable impacts of building world-class sporting facilities, and one million visitors on a town of just 18,000 and a fragile alpine ecosystem were immense:

- Ski jump: a huge concrete structure weighing thousands of tons, the ski jump was so heavy that it was in danger of sliding down the mountain. Because so much stabilising vegetation was removed, 300 reinforced concrete piles each weighing 100 tons had to be used to hold the soil in place.

- Bobsleigh run: when it was built, the locals were given gas masks in case there was a leak of ammonia, the gas used to refrigerate the $20 million run. With only 5000 registered competitors in the world, and only a fraction of those coming to the games, it was seen as unsustainable.

b) Golf

Although considered by many to be simply a pastime, golf is included as a sport because of its competitive nature. This sport is one of the most damaging to the natural environment, partly due to the fact that most courses reshape the land entirely, and partly due to the unsustainable ways in which they are managed. Currently, there are approximately 25,000 golf courses worldwide, covering an area the size of Belgium (TED, 1998). Each course undergoes a similar process, involving the clearing of vegetation, forests and creation of an artificial landscape. The environmental impacts include:

- Soil erosion leading to a loss of nutrients, exacerbated by soil compaction causing a decrease in the rate of infiltration, and an increase in overland flow.
- Use of $3000\,m^3$ water daily, or enough to meet the needs of 15,000 people.
- Large quantities of herbicides, pesticides and fertilisers that cause pollution, eutrophication, and which can also cause health problems among players, local people and workers.

The spread of golf has been phenomenal on a global scale, and it has now begun to take hold even in LEDCs such as India, Vietnam, Laos and Burma. However, the growth of golf has been most prevalent in recent years in the Far East and South-east Asia.

CASE STUDY: GOLF IN SOUTH-EAST ASIA

As golf's popularity has spread out from Japan, it has begun to bring its environmental impacts to Thailand, Indonesia, Malaysia and the Philippines. In the 1970s, South-east Asia had 45 golf courses. In 1998 there were over 500, and this figure is continuing to increase. The popularity of these courses has soared in MEDCs, as the green fees are much less expensive and, often, the courses are built in conjunction with luxury hotel developments. Golf, like skiing, is now big business, but "… the beauty found in the setting of a golf course often hides the environmental, social and health problems that environmental activists call the steep price of the game" (TED 1998).

The impacts of leisure on the natural environment

The impacts of leisure on the natural environment, similar to sporting impacts, are many and varied, but differ in that they tend to be less damaging in isolation. However, due to the popularity of countryside recreation activities, they should not be considered as less harmful in their overall effect. Hiking on a large scale, as is often seen in popular areas of the countryside of the UK, can leave lasting damage over wide areas. However, such leisure activities also highlight the common paradox of leisure, recreation and indeed tourism: that visitors and participants invariably damage or destroy the very thing they have come to enjoy. Yet, it is not only the activities themselves that are damaging. As can be seen in the next case study, the transportation of leisure seekers can cause a different type, yet equal amount, of damage to the pastime itself.

CASE STUDY: LEISURE ISSUES IN THE NATIONAL PARKS OF ENGLAND AND WALES

Currently, there are 12 National Parks in England and Wales, and two in Scotland. For the purposes of this case study, only those of England and Wales will be assessed in detail, in particular the role of traffic created by leisure pursuers. The 12 parks can be seen in Figure 28, with some miscellaneous data about each park. They were set up mostly during the 1950s, as a response to a greater desire for access to the countryside, and are still the most popular rural sites in England and Wales.

In Figure 28, the major conurbations have been added to indicate what effect the proximity of these to a park may have. The Peak National Park, as the busiest, is bounded to the north by three of the largest conurbations, so it is simple for people from these areas to make day visits. The increase in leisure time, as discussed in Chapter 4, also allows for more people to take short trips to nearby countryside sites. However, other parks such as the Lake District, Snowdonia and Pembrokeshire, while not having quite the same amount of use, are still heavily used, yet can be seen to be much further from centres of population than Northumberland, the Yorkshire Dales or the Brecon Beacons. The reasons for this are two-fold.

First, these parks have something to offer to recreational enthusiasts. The Lake District and Snowdonia offer spectacular scenery, and in Scafell and Snowdon, the highest mountains in England and Wales, respectively. Pembrokeshire offers a varied landscape, as well as many small coastal holiday resorts and beaches to rival those of Devon and Cornwall.

Secondly, since the creation of the first park, the Peak National Park in 1951, the transport network of the UK has

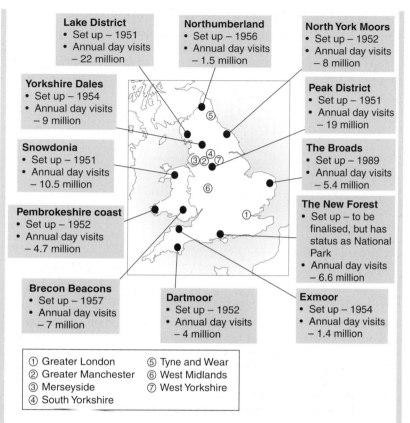

Figure 28   The 12 English and Welsh National Parks, and the seven major conurbations.

changed beyond recognition. The building of motorways and an increase in car ownership gave people a much greater personal mobility, and the ability to go where they liked, when they liked. Coupled with the decline in rural public transport services, the only feasible way to reach the countryside was by car. Linked to an increase in leisure time, this has paved the way for the catastrophic traffic problems that now blight many National Parks, whose road networks and parking facilities are simply inadequate for the number of vehicles.

According to Coalter *et al.* (1996), 91% of visitors to National Parks come by car, with only 6% by public transport or private coach trips. Their research also found that:

- Traffic was the largest single complaint of visitors to the Parks (16%).

- By 2025, traffic in the UK is projected to rise by 61–98% – with the greatest rise being seen in the countryside (perhaps up to 267%!) (Eaton and Holding, 1996).
- Twenty-five per cent of users of public transport in the parks found it unsatisfactory, hence prompting them to use their own vehicles in future.

The impacts of traffic are fairly straightforward – pollution from emissions, noise, landscape impacts and habitat disturbance to name but a few, and these can, of course, detract from the leisure experience: "… a rural road can become part of the experience of quiet enjoyment of the countryside … once it makes the transition to being a traffic road that element is lost" (Countryside Commission, 1992).

Traffic impacts in Dovedale – Peak National Park

The small limestone valley and woodland of Dovedale, with over one million visitors per year, is one of the most popular honeypot areas within the park, particularly on summer weekends and bank holidays. As a result, congestion around the area regularly occurred which detracted from the leisure experience sought by the visitors. The car park could accommodate 900 cars, but very often there was not enough room, and so people simply parked on the narrow access road, exacerbating the problem (Manley, 1991). The National Park Authority, rather than increase the size of the car park, actually decreased it, giving it a capacity of 500, hardened the paths to better cope with walkers, and stopped roadside parking by putting out large boulders to deter motorists. Now, although the number of visitors has halved, congestion is much less of a problem, as people simply have to move on elsewhere.

While this is an ideal solution for Dovedale, it actually only serves to shift the traffic problem to another area of the park. As a result, wider-reaching schemes such as park and ride, new public transport routes, positive routing of traffic to avoid congested areas and an emphasis on cycling, should all be considered to attempt to lessen the burden on the National Park's roads.

Overall, the National Parks are simply victims of their own success. They are suffering under the weight of traffic produced by the millions of visitors who come to enjoy the tranquillity, scenery and activities found in the parks each year. Solutions have been put forward for each park, but as yet there is no clear successful scheme that has been able to lessen impact of leisure traffic on the environment.

SUMMARY

- The environment includes built (urban) and natural (rural) areas, and sport and leisure can impact on both.
- Impacts on the environment can be both positive and negative.
- Impacts on the built environment very often involve the redevelopment of areas, and as a result could be considered positive impacts.
- Impacts on the natural environment often involve overuse or inappropriate use, and could therefore be considered negative impacts.
- Economic considerations may come before environmental ones, and so impacts occur whether desired or not.
- Management of the natural environment can help to alleviate negative impacts, but these still occur even in protected areas such as National Parks.

Questions

1. For one further completed urban redevelopment scheme for sport or leisure that you have studied, assess the impacts this has had on the built environment.
2. For one proposed redevelopment schemes in your town or city, answer the following questions:
   a) what are the issues?
   b) what are the costs and benefits?
   c) what are peoples' opinions of the proposals?
3. Using an atlas and Figure 28, assess the accessibility of the National Parks in England and Wales to the wider population:
   a) to what extent does the road network help or hinder leisure seekers?
   b) does the proximity to large areas of population have a bearing on numbers of visitors?
4. For an outdoor activity you are interested in:
   a) where are the most popular areas in which it is carried out – is there a similarity between them?
   b) what are the impacts on **one** specific area of your chosen activity?
   c) how can these impacts be managed effectively?

6 Sport, Leisure and Existing Inequalities

The differences in sport and leisure pursuits between wealthy more economically developed countries (MEDCs), newly industrialising countries (NICs) and poorer less economically developed countries (LEDCs) are often marked, and have been touched on in previous chapters. Chapter 2 has given some detail on the differences in terms of the economic status of countries, but only in terms of countries becoming 'hotspots' for particular sports, whether through major developments or for other reasons. In this particular chapter, there will be an assessment of these differences in more detail, and the ways in which the level of development of a country can affect the quality and range of sporting or leisure activities within it. Coupled to this, there will be an appraisal of patterns of sporting migration, with reference to the economic push and pull factors that cause sportsmen and women to migrate, in general, from LEDCs to MEDCs, or from a poorer 'south' to a richer 'north', rather than necessarily to 'hotspots'.

1 Measures of Development

The term development is measurable in many ways, and it is necessary to define exactly what are meant by MEDCs and LEDCs in this context. There are several different criteria which, when compared, give some idea as to how a country may be classified. The discriminators assessed here are: the Brandt Line (north–south divide), gross domestic product (GDP) and the United Nations Development Programme (UNDP) measure of human development index (HDI). Each of these has their merits and problems, as identified in the following section. In relation to sport, it will be seen that they are also able to provide a certain insight into the reasons why particular countries have more or less provision and participation than others.

a) The Brandt Line

In 1980, Willy Brandt, the former Chancellor of West Germany, chaired the Commission on International Development that aimed to identify which countries were more developed, and which were less. The Commission came up with the Brandt Line, better known as the north–south divide, which essentially divided the world in two (see Figure 29). Those countries to the north of the line were considered to be richer and more developed, while those to the south were seen as poorer, and less developed. Of course, this overview of the world situation was an over-simplification, but it gave some idea as to how the world was divided. Yet, today it may no longer be as relevant as it once was.

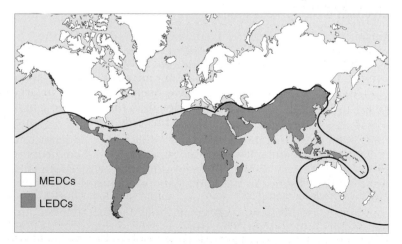

Figure 29   The Brandt Line: the theoretical divide between the rich 'north' and the poor 'south'.

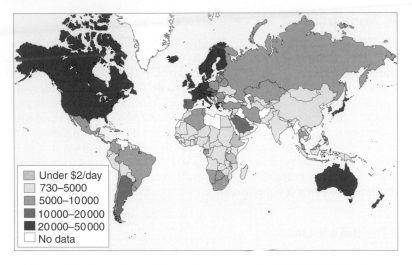

Figure 30 Gross domestic product per capita (2000) in US dollars.

b) Gross domestic product

Gross domestic product, or GDP, is a measure of the economic development of a country, calculating the total value of all goods and services produced in a country in a year, and is usually (as in Figure 30), divided by the total population to give a per capita figure. This estimates a country's level of development, but it only accounts for the economy: social, political and environmental aspects are not considered.

c) Human development index

Human development index, or HDI, is a measure devised by the UNDP to try and give an overall measure of development, in recognition of the shortcomings of the other two measures. It combines data from various sources, and attempts to give each country a score, out of 1, depending on how far they have to go to attain certain goals: an average life span of 85 years, access to education for all and a decent income (see Figure 31).

It is plain to see that the Brandt Line, while simple and easy to use, is now probably too much of an over-generalisation. Some countries below the line, such as Singapore, South Africa and South Korea, should not be classified as the same as poor countries such as Sierra Leone and Niger. The GDP measure, while a good indicator of the economic development of a country, is limited in that it does not take other factors into account. Therefore, for the purposes of this book, the HDI, a composite measure based on a combination of several relevant factors, will be used to help identify and explain development at

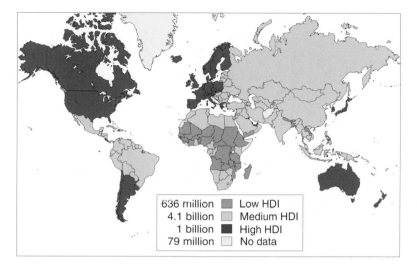

636 million ▨ Low HDI
4.1 billion ▢ Medium HDI
1 billion ▮ High HDI
79 million ▢ No data

Figure 31 Human development index: based on a variety of economic, social and environmental factors.

three main levels, as shown on Figure 31. Thus, the MEDCs (or MDCs, using the HDI) have a high HDI, LEDCs (LDCs) have a low HDI and those in the middle can be thought of as newly industrialising countries (NICs) or emerging market countries (EMCs). These two latter terms refer to countries that could no longer be considered to be the poorest or least developed, but have not quite become fully developed. The UNDP uses all of these terms to identify a particular country's status.

2 Level of Development and Sport: An Overview

So why is development relevant to sport? Surely the enjoyment of physical activity is something for all people around the world? This would be the case in an ideal world, but it would be naïve to think that this was the actual pattern. The level of development of a country affects all facets of life, with sport as one area that particularly suffers with a low level of development.

A general overview of the situation can be seen in Table 14, which summarises the case for each different type of country. Bear in mind, this is not necessarily true for all countries – it is merely a guide to the situation.

Table 14 gives some idea of the differences between countries of different levels of development. The evidence for much of this

Table 14 Comparison of global sport and leisure situations

	MEDC	LEDC	NIC/EMC
Sports facilities	Modern, extensive range Access for majority of population Many large-scale events Sporting bodies set up to run a structured system of amateur and professional sports	Few specific sporting facilities: may often be disused or misused Low priority given to sporting facilities Lack of government investment in new facilities Disorganised and fragmented approach to sports organisation	New facilities built in drive to development High technology used to make modern facilities Disorganisation as far as sports system concerned: new set up with little expertise
Leisure facilities	Large range of home-based and away from home opportunities for leisure Technology plays a major part in many pastimes	Few specific facilities dedicated to leisure Little technological expertise leads to simple pastimes	Modern facilities available for a wide cross-section of society Advancement in technology allows facilities to rival MEDCs
Leisure time	Increasing leisure time allows for more opportunities for leisure Travel for leisure pastimes	Low levels of leisure time Time mostly spent working towards survival Leisure time involves mostly community or home-based, family activities	Time for leisure beginning to increase Work ethic still very prevalent: leads to lack of opportunity Constraints on time mean many new facilities unused
Disposable income	More money to spend on sport and leisure goods for individuals	Lack of disposable income leads to low ability to pay for leisure Money used to pay for basic needs	As income increases, leisure opportunities increase

can be found in Section 3 of this chapter. However, an example of the types of countries can be seen when applying sports facilities to them.

MEDC: UK

- Sporting facilities such as stadia are common throughout the country, and at the top are built to a very high standard, both of comfort and safety.
- The government put sport as a priority, as shown by the willingness to bid for the 2012 Olympic games.
- Each sport has its own regulating, governing body, and Sport England, the national organisation for sport, oversees the whole system.

LEDC: Afghanistan

- Very few large-scale facilities. The National Stadium in Kabul was used for public beheadings under the deposed Taliban regime, and is in a state of disrepair.
- International participation almost non-existent. A female athlete was allowed to compete in the 100 m for the first time at the 2002 World Athletics Championships.

NIC: Malaysia

- Modern facilities built for the 1998 Commonwealth Games in Kuala Lumpur. Helped to raise the profile of the country – now get little international use.
- New Formula 1 Sepang Circuit considered to be one of the most advanced in the world.
- Sports governing bodies have been set up, but are disorganised and fragmented, with little expertise.

3 The Measurement of Sporting Difference: The Development Dilemma

Sporting and leisure development in MEDCs has had detailed appraisal in previous chapters, so it is now the turn of LEDCs. Sports events and access to more sporting facilities may be the goal of some LEDCs, but, ultimately, they cannot be seen as a substitute to basic human needs. The slogan "No queremos goles, queremos frijoles", meaning "We do not want goals, we want beans", was painted on the wall of a Mexico Stadium during the 1986 Football World Cup, and it sums up the development dilemma in LEDCs.

Unsurprisingly, if sport is studied in relation to the level of development, it is plain to see that the lower the level of economic development, the less sport practice, performance, facilities and finance are developed (Andreff, 2000). As a result, many countries suffer a 'brawn drain' of their most talented athletes to more economically developed countries. The effects of this migration will be appraised later in this chapter. Yet, it is almost impossible to assess exactly how much of an effect low development has on a country, as there is little specific data from these countries – in itself, an indicator of a low level of development. However, UNESCO did send a questionnaire to certain LEDCs, with some startling results (detailed in Andreff, 2000) as shown in the following case study.

CASE STUDY: SPORTING ISSUES IN LEDCS

Sport in education

Education is one of the main sources of sporting experience, and in MEDCs, where primary enrolment is 99% or higher, exposure to different sport forms is part of the curriculum. However, in Eritrea the enrolment rate is 30%, 28% in Ethiopia and Mali, and in Niger the rate is 25%. This automatically means that children in these countries have less than one-third of the probability of being exposed to sport. Yet, even when exposure does occur, the ratio of children to teacher (40–100 per teacher) means that the experience is likely to be fragmented and insufficient.

Individual sports participation

Within Europe, affiliation to sports organisations is between 20 and 25%, strict sport participation rate is 21–48%, and general, *ad hoc* participation is 54–82% (Andreff, 2000). Within African LEDCs, rates are far lower, on average being 0.0013% for affiliations, and between 0.0007 and 1.4% for participation. Also, 'sophisticated' sports requiring specific technologies (cycling, motor racing, swimming, golf) are almost non-existent – sports participated in tend to be simple and non-technologically advanced such as athletics, football, basketball or martial arts.

Investment in sport

In most LEDCs, the government is the chief investor and supporter of national sport, but has a duty to improve the standard of living of its people at the same time. As a result, sport is given a lower priority for funding, and so causes a huge international disparity in terms of the level of sporting success. The Olympic Games are a prime example of the gulf between MEDCs and NICs and LEDCs. In poorer countries, talented Olympic athletes do not have equal chances of successful participation, because they cannot afford the same financial and material support for training and preparation, except in those sports (such as track events) that require only hard work, and little in the way of specialist facilities. Figure 32 brings the development gap between MEDCs and LEDCs into sharp focus.

Figure 32 shows quite clearly that there is a huge difference between the performance of MEDCs and LEDCs. In fact, not only is the number of medals won by MEDCs much larger, it is also concentrated in many fewer countries. For example, in Atlanta 1996, the MEDC/Former USSR group numbered 46 nations, whereas the LEDC group numbered 151! Also, the medals won by LEDCs are concentrated in a very few sports. Eighty per cent of all the medals won by African countries are in athletics (and running in particular) and boxing. Asian countries specialise in martial arts, racket sports and boxing, and South America in football and tennis – in other words, relatively low-technology events.

One interesting anomaly would be the former USSR. While its HDI is in the middle group (Figure 31), and it had a GDP comparable to many South American countries, it did have great success. This is due in the main to intensive state funding. Sport was an international battleground where political points could be scored against the Western nations. Before the 1984 Los Angeles Olympics, the USSR and Eastern Europe dominated many sports. Now, they still perform well, but the priorities in the infant democracies have had to shift, at the expense of much of the previously available sports funding.

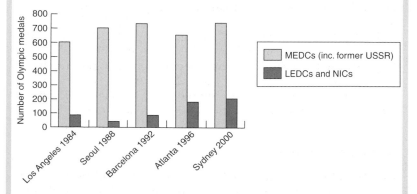

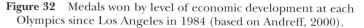

Figure 32   Medals won by level of economic development at each Olympics since Los Angeles in 1984 (based on Andreff, 2000).

Lack of major world sports events

Approximately 30 MEDCs organise and host about 95% of all major world sporting events, for the simple reason of expense. Those few events that do find their way into LEDCs or NICs are usually heavily sponsored from abroad. Only large NICs such as Mexico (1986 Football World Cup), Malaysia (1998 Commonwealth Games) or South Korea (1988 Olympics, joint hosts of 2002 Football World Cup) have really had any effective involvement in staging world events.

Overall, then, LEDCs and even the improving NICs still have a long way to go to catch up with the powerful and dominant MEDCs in the world of sports, and not just in major events. At all levels, LEDCs suffer from a lack of funding and facilities. As a result, many highly talented athletes find themselves travelling around the globe, plying their trade in countries other than their own and, in some exceptional circumstances, will even adopt another country as their own in order to perform at the highest level. This migration of sportsmen and women, the so-called 'brawn drain' is detailed in the next section, which looks at different migrant typologies, and gives examples from the worlds of athletics and football.

4 Sports Migration and the 'Brawn Drain' (Muscle Drain)

Migration for the purpose of both sport and leisure is a common occurrence. Sportsmen and women travel around the world seeking to compete in events in their sport, that often end up in diverse and exotic locations. Migration for leisure, on the other hand, is basically tourism, which will not be covered in any depth in this book. It is important to note that sportsmen and women who travel can be considered as business tourists, as they fit into the definition given at the beginning of this chapter.

Migration is defined by Guinness (2002) as: "... the movement of people across a specified boundary, national or international, to establish a new permanent place of residence. The United Nations define permanent as a change of residence lasting more than one year". This is a concise definition that is entirely relevant to some, but not all sports participants. The nature of sport means that often migration is short term, with many such movements occurring in a short space of time. However, it is entirely applicable to migrants from LEDCs travelling to MEDCs for work.

Sports migration is very much a part of the globalisation process that is currently occurring in sport, a process that will be assessed in more detail in Chapter 7. However, in itself, migration takes on two forms – in the search for competition, and in the search for employment overseas. The difference between these two is subtle. The former may well be a requirement for an athlete to prove his or her prowess, by travelling to where their events are taking place, whereas the latter is more likely to be seeking to perform at the highest level abroad, simply because the level of a sport in their home country is too low. Thus, the 'brawn drain' occurs, as talented athletes from LEDCs look for employment in the wealthy, rewarding MEDCs.

a) Migrant typologies

Maguire (1999) and Bale (2000) both give details of different migrant types, all of which will be assessed here. They include both those who seek to perform at the highest level wherever their sport takes them, or simply travel to where they will receive better pay.

The dimensionality of these typologies can be seen in Figure 33.

Nomadic cosmopolitans

The nomadic cosmopolitans could perhaps be considered the sporting purists, those who travel for the love of the sporting experience, and use their sport as an excuse to travel. Examples of this could be marathon runners, extreme sports enthusiasts or skiers and surfboarders. They are not necessarily motivated by financial gain, but travel and stay in places for short times to broaden their experiences.

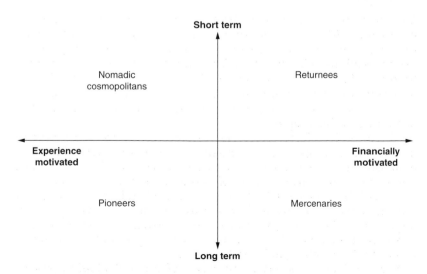

Figure 33 Dimensionality of sporting migrant typologies.

Pioneers

The pioneers are a relatively rare group these days. The idea of extolling the virtues of one's sporting ethos, such as the nineteenth century missionaries bringing rugby to the Pacific, and cricket to the Caribbean. Again, not financially motivated, but keen to initiate and convert those who have not experienced their particular sport form.

Returnees

The returnees can be considered the sporting professional who must travel the world in order to compete in the various different competitions set up for his or her sport form. These can include rally drivers, Formula 1 drivers, professional golfers and professional tennis players, all of who have to travel to compete with the best in the world, and reap the financial rewards. They are continually on the move, but between events they will return home to train and rest, until forced to travel again.

Mercenaries

As the name suggests, mercenaries are motivated to participate in sport for purely financial gain, and settle in a different country or region to play their sport at possibly a higher level than is available in their own country. Footballers are a prime example of this, as when they are employed abroad they must live there for a longer term, in order to play throughout the season, and for the number of years on their contracts. In extreme cases, mercenaries may become settlers or even citizens of the country, particularly if their chosen sport has little or no funding in their own country.

In the context of this chapter, it is the last group of migrants who are the most relevant, as they are the ones seeking to gain financial reward, as well as play at the highest level, by moving to another country. Sportsmen and women from LEDCs have become recent economic migrants, as the facilities and organisations cannot be found in their home countries.

CASE STUDY: FOOTBALL, EUROPE AND THE 'BRAWN DRAIN'

Andreff (2003) has made studies of the 'brawn drain' of the most talented players from developing countries. He concluded that there is evidence of the brawn drain from LEDCs to European countries, to play football in particular. This also occurs in the USA, but in baseball, in ice hockey and in basketball. Two main reasons are given:

1. The wage gap between developing and developed countries (professional sports) triggers players' international mobility.

2. Moreover, not enough physical education, sport participation, coaches, state and municipality sport budgets and sport facilities are available in developing countries.

These factors have given rise to an enormous increase in the number of overseas footballers playing in Europe. While within Europe there is great fluidity of movement – the English Premier League, for example, attracts large numbers of French, Dutch and Scandinavian players – there are also a large number of players from outside Europe, most notably from Africa (see Figure 34) and South America, all of whom come as mercenary migrants.

Figure 34 shows just how many African players found a way out of poverty, and into the richest football leagues in the world. France, in particular, has been a beneficiary of many top players, due to the number of former colonies they scoured for talent. As

Number of migrants

150   100   50   20   10   1

Figure 34   African professional footballers in Europe (adapted from Bale, 2003 and source data of Ricci, 2000).

a result of this 'cherry-picking', players were offered lucrative deals to move abroad. Some players, such as Patrick Viera (Senegal) and Marcel Desailly (Ghana), even gave up their nationalities to be able to represent their new homes. Conversely, a few such as Freddie Kanoute (France – Mali) have given up their nationalities in order to represent their ancestral African countries!

Darby (2001) gives some details of the growth in the numbers of African players in Europe. He states that by the mid-1990s there were some 350 Africans in European first and second divisions. By 2000, this number had risen to 770, with 145 more playing in lower leagues. This can partly be explained by the success of countries such as Nigeria and Cameroon in the Olympics (1996 and 2000 gold medal winners, respectively), and the fact that labour from Africa is much cheaper than home-grown talent, or other European players.

To break this trend down further, it is possible to study the numbers of both African and South American footballers playing in the English Premier League. Figure 35 shows the numbers and origin of many players, but includes one or two players, such as those mentioned above, who have committed themselves to a new country, and a new nationality. They are also represented on the map.

The total number of African and South American players in Premiership squads at the start of 2004 was 64, with 36 coming from Africa, and 28 from South America (including the Caribbean). Most of these players come from reasonably successful footballing nations in international terms, such as Nigeria and Cameroon, as well as Brazil and Argentina. Yet, it is interesting to note that countries whose teams made it to the World Cup Finals in Japan and South Korea in 2002 are also beginning to be represented, such as Senegal and Jamaica. This could be because they have finally come to the attention of the big English clubs, after international exposure at the highest level.

The 'brawn drain' from Africa in particular is sometimes argued as being a good thing for African football. The players are playing at the top level, are gaining a good income and have opportunities they would not otherwise have in their own countries. Yet, according to Darby (2001), opponents of the current situation argue that standards of play amongst those left in their domestic leagues are reduced, reducing media and spectator attention, and also creating difficulties when European clubs refuse to release players for international duty. It is a situation that has remarkable similarities to the colonial period, when European countries exploited the wealth and resources of many African countries. Now it is not the wealth, but the talent that is being exploited.

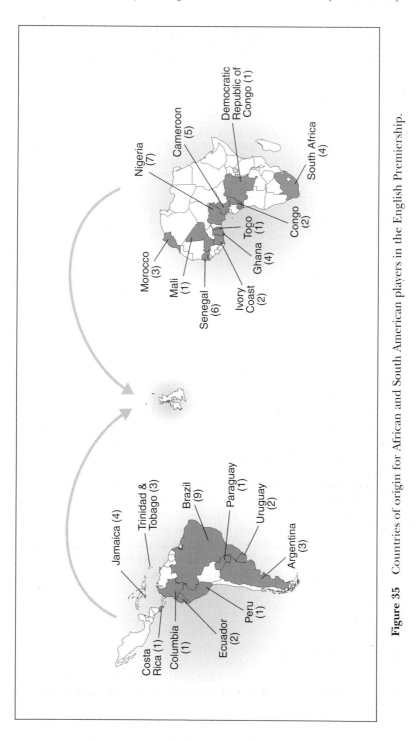

Figure 35 Countries of origin for African and South American players in the English Premiership.

CASE STUDY: THE LURE OF MONEY IN ATHLETICS

The previous case study dealt with the mercenary migrant typology, but only in the sense that footballers moved abroad to play at the highest level, and earn good wages. Sometimes, they would even change their nationality to be able to play for a successful nation. However, in one sport in particular, some athletes have gone one step further: they have simply changed allegiance for money.

In the world of athletics, there are several cases of athletes changing their nationality, not for the glory of the country or to perform for a successful nation, but to earn better money than they could in their native countries. And once again, understandably, the majority of these athletes are from LEDCs, moving to MEDCs, although this trend is also changing, as we shall see.

Examples of some of these athletes include Wilson Kipketer, a distance runner formerly of Kenya but now running for Denmark; Eunice Barber, born in Sierra Leone but winning a long jump gold medal for France; and Moroccan born Khalid Khannouchi, made a US citizen in 2000 and a record-holder by 2002 (Skari, 2003). In fact, according to Istvan Gyulai, the International Amateur Athletics Federation General Secretary, there have been over 60 requests for 'transfer of allegiance' since 2001. Yet, these examples all cite athletes moving from LEDCs to MEDCs. Some are now moving to new countries not previously thought as MEDCs, but which are immensely wealthy.

For example, in 2003, Saif Saeed Shaheen, formerly known as Stephen Cherono, defected from Kenya to run for Qatar, for a guaranteed $1000 per month for life. Although this is hardly a fortune, Kenyans competing for their own country can expect less than $400 per year. Shaheen openly admits he moved for the money, to join former Sudanese runner Kamis Abdullah Saifeldin in running for Qatar. Saifeldin earned around $180,000 in bonuses alone in 2002 (Williams, 2003). Overall, such moves are officially frowned on, but appear to be another feature of the widening gap between the rich north and poor south.

SUMMARY

- The level of development of countries varies, and can be measured in a variety of different ways.
- The existence of a development gap between the north and the south has led to a difference in sport and leisure priorities between countries.

- Sport and leisure can be used to identify the level of economic development that a country has attained.
- Level of development affects sports provision, participation, and levels of achievement and excellence.
- Sports migration occurs all over the world, both within and between countries, and for a variety of motivations.
- As a result of the development gap between rich and poor countries, migration is often seen as a 'muscle drain' or 'brawn drain' as talented sports men and women from poorer countries seek their fortunes in wealthier countries.
- Africa in particular has seen a huge exodus of footballers to Europe, and the exploitation of this talent is causing domestic problems for the nations that they have left.
- Athletes from poorer countries have begun to change their nationalities to be able to earn greater income running for another country.

Questions

1. Using Table 14 to help, choose one MEDC, one LEDC and one NIC, and discuss the extent to which their levels of development can account for the provision of large-scale sporting facilities found there.
2. Economic development studies have in recent years only just started to assess the disparity in sports provision between LEDCs and MEDCs. Why might this have been a neglected area in the past?
3. Use Figure 32 as a basis for a short report into the success of a range of contrasting countries in any sporting competition. For example, you could assess the differences in levels of development between countries in the Football World Cup, tennis players in a Grand Slam competition, or an athletics event. Look back over the years to see what patterns emerge, and attempt to explain them.
4. Attempt to account for the patterns shown in Figure 35. How might a similar diagram, based around players in the UK from Asian countries, differ?
5. "The practice of athletes changing allegiance from one country to another should be banned." To what extent do you agree with this statement?

7 Sporting Futures

"We want to see everyone given a better sporting future ... so that the power of sport can be available to all, and so that the passion of sport can continue to move us and engage us and be part of our lives. Sport matters."

Tony Blair, UK Prime Minister (2000)

In essence, this quotation sums up the issues to be covered in this final chapter. It will assess the current state of sport in its global context, and in particular the process of globalisation and its impact on sport. It will also study alternative strategies that may allow sport to develop in a sustainable manner, and whether 'sport for all' is an aim that can be realistically achieved.

1 The Process of Globalisation

The process of globalisation has been rapid, and over the past few years it has continued at a phenomenal rate. However, its roots can be traced back many centuries, to the Europe of the early fifteenth century. Robertson (1992) actually perceives the globalisation process as occurring in five distinct phases (see Figure 36), all of which contain individual characteristics, but all of which have worked towards the homogenising of the modern world.

In terms of leisure, the role of transnational corporations (TNCs) now mirrors that of the early colonial countries – powerful bodies desiring an increase in the size of their 'empire' (or in this case market), leading to an homogeneity in terms of goods and services. In the case of sports, that role could potentially be seen as being filled by the media, whose influence has spread the sporting message across the globe with the aid of satellites, the Internet, radio and television.

Figure 36 gives a very brief, basic outline of what the general global trends have been over the course of the past 550 years, but it is really the last phase that is the most important for the context of this chapter. The uncertainty phase is well named, as it is difficult, in the case of sport, to see exactly what the future holds. Is the best policy to follow the lead made by globalisation, or would locally based schemes be more sustainable?

Phase 1	1450s	Germinal phase: period when growth of national communities occurred and ideas about humanity and a scientific world-view emerged.
Phase 2	1750s	Incipient phase: the notion of an homogenous, single state developed, and standardisation of various notions occurred, such as human rights and legal conventions on international trade.
Phase 3	1870s	Take-off phase: growth of world-wide agencies, global competitions and standardisations of most concepts of human rights.
Phase 4	1920s	Struggle for hegemony phase: period of global mistrust and polarisation, characterised by the Cold War between the West and the Soviet Bloc. Sporting rivalries mirrored political ones.
Phase 5	1980s	Uncertainty phase: huge increase in the number of global institutions, and in the multicultural nature of more societies. Both these phenomena have caused problems, as the world becomes smaller, and homogeneity increases.

Figure 36 The history of the globalisation process (after Robertson quoted in Maguire, 1999).

2 Sport and the Globalisation Process: The Role of the Media

The globalisation of sport has been very much facilitated by the growth of the media, in particular television and satellite technology. A network of satellites that can beam information to anywhere in the world now surrounds the globe, and areas that can receive these signals have a choice of hundreds of television channels to watch. Because of this network, sport has been one of the most successful cross-cultural transfers, owing to the fact that the nature of most sports or games are instantly recognisable as competitions that arouse interest in the observer.

The role of television both in the domestic market, and across the globe cannot be underestimated. Since the 1960s, the main objectives for most professional sports have been the gaining of and increase in revenue from lucrative television contracts. The leaps forward in technology have enabled many diverse sports to be presented and marketed away from the traditional 'live' spectators (Whitson, 1998). Replays and camera work have further augmented the experience of the armchair enthusiast, and in recent years the development of digital television has allowed for the development of interactive statistics,

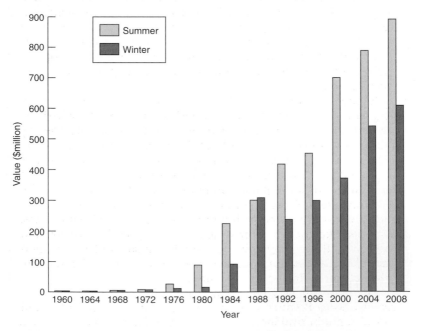

Figure 37   Amount by US television companies for rights to televise the Olympics in the USA.

and 'player-cams', where the viewer can choose to focus on one player in a team sport.

Over the years, professional sports have begun to rely on television revenues and sponsorship deals in order be able to pay increasingly large wage bills and facility maintenance costs. Yet, television companies actively compete for the rights to televise sporting events in order to monopolise certain sectors of the market. As a result, the price of television rights has increased dramatically, as Figure 37 shows. Three major US television networks, CBS, NBC and ABC, have bid almost exclusively for the rights to air the Olympics, both summer and winter, since 1960, to such an extent that they are now almost single-handedly funding the Olympics.

CASE STUDY: SATELLITE TELEVISION AND PREMIERSHIP FOOTBALL

The Olympics are not the only sporting area to gain financially from the media. English football has been another area to receive lucrative deals from television companies. In the late 1980s, the top clubs (Division 1 as it was then known) felt that the system of television rights in English football was unfair, and that television revenues to Spanish and Italian clubs meant that while they were boosted, the English clubs fell behind. An egalitarian system of collective rights was in place, where the clubs from all four divisions had money from television rights shared evenly among them. This meant that the lower-placed, less-popular clubs were receiving a boost on the back of the popularity of the major clubs.

In 1992, the top 20 clubs broke away to form the Premiership, and with the advent of satellite television in 1989, they had the perfect opportunity to negotiate an exclusive deal with the Sky television company. Not only has this dramatically increased football revenues, but it has also meant that subscribers to Sky increased from two million in 1992 to six million in 1998. The percentages of subscribing households can be seen in Figure 38. The increase in football revenues can be seen in Figure 39. This increase has greatly contributed to the turnover of major clubs, such as Manchester United and Arsenal, both directly and indirectly, through greater sponsorship deals and global merchandising. As a result, audiences are now not just confined to the UK, but can be found all over the world.

The figures from 1992 onwards were all paid by Sky, for exclusive access to Premier League matches. Although the BBC and ITV also put in rival bids, they could not afford to match the bids of Sky. However, by this time the issue was not just a national one. The rights purchased by Sky allowed them to broadcast across

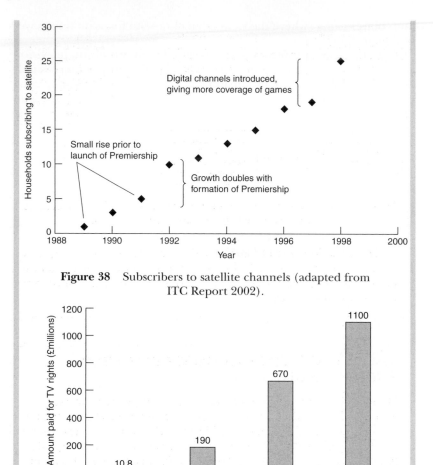

Figure 38 Subscribers to satellite channels (adapted from ITC Report 2002).

Figure 39 Total amount paid by television companies for football rights.

the globe, which has led to the Premiership being the most popular national football league in the world. This has in turn led to the immense growth of clubs such as Manchester United.

One further consequence of the injection of money, and hence the globalisation of the game, has been what many have seen as the unsustainable inflation of football's economy, especially in terms of player wages and transfer fees. Major European clubs, such as Leeds and Real Madrid, have struggled to be able to cope with these spiralling costs. Figure 40 gives an impression of why this has occurred.

Figure 40 Flow diagram to demonstrate the contribution of increased television revenues to football's economic crisis.

The situation has got even further out of control, and, as a result, clubs have sought more diverse sources of finance, including sponsorship, merchandising and specific media development (e.g. Manchester United TV).

CASE STUDY: THE MANCHESTER UNITED PHENOMENON

Manchester United is one of the largest and perhaps best-known football clubs in the world. Its annual turnover has been steadily increasing over the years (see Figure 41), as it becomes a true product of globalisation. Much of this increase in turnover is due to an increase in television revenue, particularly after the inception of satellite television and the Premiership.

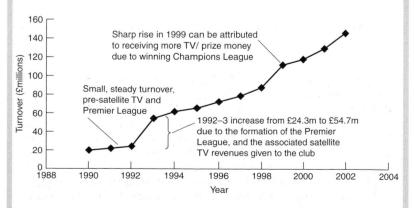

Figure 41 Increase in Manchester United's turnover, 1990–2002.

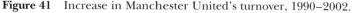

Global fame – Manchester United are possibly the best-known club in the world. 79% of people have heard of them, and according to their own research they are the best-supported club in the world, with a 39% share. Juventus, in second place, could only manage 4%. Sophisticated marketing and a popularity based on glamour, have given them an estimated worth of over £1 billion. Glamorous players also play an important part.

USA market – Within the USA, Manchester United have struggled to find a market foothold. The reason for this is partly due to the fact that football is by no means the most popular, or closely followed, sport in america, despite the hosting of the 1994 World Cup. In an effort to tap into the lucrative American market, they have negotiated sponsorship deals with large American firms such as Pepsi and Budweiser, and have also bough a stake in the New York Yankees baseball team, in an effort to promote themselves to a wider, yet discerning sports audience.

The Far East market – Traditionally, Manchester United have had a long association with supporters in the Far East. Malaysia in particular has a dedicated following in the aftermath of the country being a part of the British Empire. As a result, merchandise shops and the 'Red Café' have been opened in Kuala Lumpur, as well as Singapore. A tour to China, Malaysia, Singapore and Thailand in 2001 boosted their image, and the fact that 3 o'clock kick off times in the UK coincides with prime time evening TV scheduling has kept their profile high.

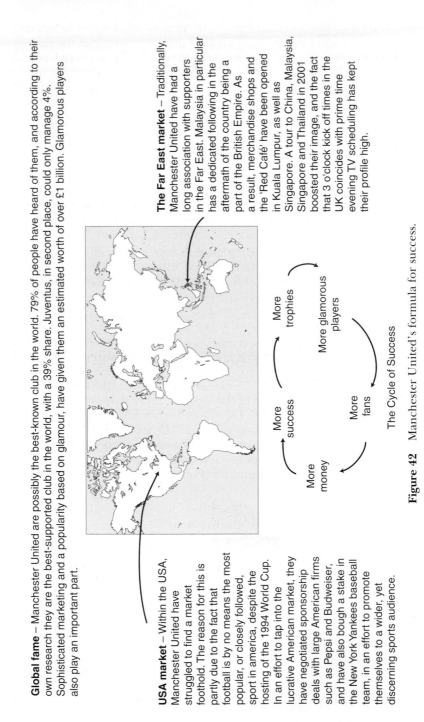

The Cycle of Success

More success → More trophies → More glamorous players → More fans → More money →

Figure 42 Manchester United's formula for success.

Much of the financial success of Manchester United is based around match receipts and media payments, but, also, its wide global appeal has led to a lucrative sideline in commercial payments. Figure 42 gives a picture of the kind of appeal Manchester United has around the globe, and why this has led to such a lucrative commercial turnover. The cycle of success depicted in this figure also shows how Manchester United have been able to make purchases of players to boost success on the back of previous footballing success, and in successfully marketing the club worldwide. Figure 43 shows how the revenue of the club is divided between its different facets.

It indicates that while Manchester United gain almost half their revenue from gate receipts and television rights, another third is attributable to merchandising. And it is this successful marketing of the club as a product that has helped the club to grow, and reach more and more diverse regions of the world.

The final piece in the success of the club is the glamour aspect that it has developed. As well as being extremely successful, it has marketed its image as a 'sexy' club, with a plethora of football 'stars' over the years such as Dennis Law, George Best, Eric Cantona, Ryan Giggs and, most recently (although controversially no more), David Beckham. The latter took this glamour to another level, with his marriage to 'Posh Spice' Victoria Adams, an international star in her own right. Many would argue that with his move to Real Madrid, the global interest is beginning to shift towards Spain.

Of course, Manchester United is not the only club to have used globalisation to its advantage. Arsenal have websites devoted to different areas of the world (e.g. http://asia.arsenal.com),

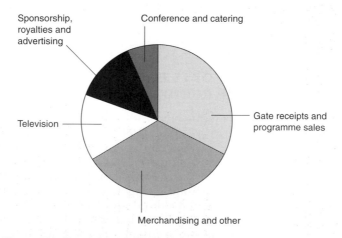

Figure 43   Breakdown of Manchester United's turnover.

and Everton saw the opportunity for sponsorship from abroad – the Chinese electronics firm Keijan sponsored them for £2 million over 2 years, and they do not even sell products in the UK! They were simply taking advantage of interest from the Asian market.

3 The Sport and Leisure Goods Industry and the Globalisation Process

The sport and leisure goods industry has also benefited greatly from globalisation, although it could be argued that their contribution has been less than positive. The situation is that much of the industry is dominated by TNCs who, while offering employment in many LEDCs around the world, have been alleged by some people to treat their workers poorly. They are attracted to countries such as India, China and Bangladesh by low wage bills, tax incentives from governments and, allegedly, take advantage of unsophisticated employers' codes of practice in such countries. As a result, it has been reported that some firms pay less than minimum wages, force their workers to work excessively long hours and, in some cases, even use child labour (see www.labourbehindthelabel.org for further discussion).

The case study looks at the types of conditions and situations that many workers in LEDCs find themselves in, and how things are beginning to change. TNCs in general are assessed to see how their work practices have caused public outcry. It must be stressed, however, that not all TNCs fall into this category, and that some have entered into initiatives with the Fairtrade Labelling Organisation (FLO) to give workers on sports equipment and other, often agricultural products, a fair deal.

CASE STUDY: SPORTS EQUIPMENT MANUFACTURE IN INDIA

The sporting goods industry in India is long established, going back well over 100 years. Since 1947, and the partitioning of India and Pakistan, the sporting goods industry has settled in Jalandhar and Meerut (see Figure 44). Over the past 50 years, it has experienced phenomenal growth, and is extremely important to the Indian economy owing to the intensive labour it requires. The goods manufactured are distributed to many different places around the world, taking advantage of a developed world hungry for sporting equipment (www.sporting-goods-industry.com).

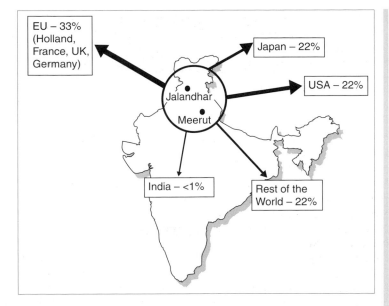

Figure 44   The location and market for the Indian sporting goods industry.

Sports goods have grown up to become roughly 100 major industries and 20,000 small-scale industries in Jalandhar alone. These factories produce 318 different sports items, which are distributed as shown in Figure 44. This merchandise is then also distributed and sold at a fair price through the efforts of the Sports Goods Export Promotion Council (SGEPC), an international body affiliated to European, Asian and US sports goods industries. Set up in 1958, they promote the export of sporting goods from India (www.hunttech.com/sgepc/profile.htm). Because of its established global pedigree, the Indian sports goods industry is flourishing, although it does have its downside.

As a result of the prominence of the industry through the process of globalisation, it has come to the attention of MEDCs that many items, such as those that require small stitching (shuttlecocks, cricket balls, etc.), are manufactured by poorly paid child labourers, whose hands are small enough to make light work of this. Thus, charities such as the South Asian Coalition on Child Servitude (SACCS) have targeted the industry to try and negotiate better wages and/or the assigning of child work to adults (more often than not, women). SACCS also set up two schools to educate children taken from the industry (www.saccsweb.org). As a result of work by such charities, children are given a better start in life, while the sports goods industry in India continues to make high-quality sports merchandise.

4 TNCs and the Global Sport and Leisure Market

TNCs have grown enormously over the past 100 years, both driving and thriving off the process of globalisation. They are generally immensely powerful, particularly in economic terms, and the sport and leisure industry is no exception. Much of this wealth, it is alleged by critics of globalisation, has been built on exploitation of workers in LEDCs, in much the same way as already mentioned in the India sports goods industry case study. Yet, many charities and anti-globalisation groups would argue that sport- and leisure-based companies such as the well-known brands in the market have made little or no effort to improve conditions for their suppliers' workers and continue to allow exploitation. There is a wide range of resources available on the Internet, of varying degrees of accuracy, that paint a very stark picture of the influence of these TNCs (www.labourbehindthelabel.org, www.caa.org.au/campaigns/nike/appear to be more balanced than some). Globalisation, while a good thing in terms of sharing of cultures, information and ideas, has perhaps also enabled unethical working practices to take place in LEDCs who cannot turn down the offer of foreign investment.

Therefore, it may be pertinent to ask the question: 'How sustainable is globalisation in sport and leisure, and is there an alternative?'. The first part is hard to answer, although the evidence provided here suggests not. Footballing wages, transfer prices and television deals, for example, surely cannot increase indefinitely, and yet the popularity of Manchester United shows no signs of declining as satellite television reaches out to more and more people. In the same way, unethical working practices are unlikely to last for ever in LEDCs, and, as shown in India, they are making a success of the sports goods industry while reforming working practices.

The second part does have a more obvious answer: the small-scale, local, grass-roots approach. However, this is more appropriate when associated with the provision of sport and leisure, rather than global production of sport and leisure goods. The former could be seen as more altruistic, and therefore easier to maintain sustainably. But with the latter, as long as there is a profit to be made, there is always the opportunity for exploitation.

5 Small-scale, Sustainable Sport and Leisure: The Role of the Grass-roots Approach

For many countries, the provision of sport and leisure opportunities is based around the ability of the individual to pay (see Chapter 1). But there are definite moves afoot, both in MEDCs and LEDCs, to try to include more people in sport, and allow in particular the disadvantaged to be able to enjoy it. Providing sporting opportunities in this way clearly requires a great deal of organisation, and thus in LEDCs, in particular, outside assistance is often required. The case studies below detail the grass-roots approaches in both MEDCs and LEDCs, and it can be seen that there are many similarities between the two, because of the characteristics of the target population. According to Torkildsen (1992), there are five different factors that influence people's ability to access leisure; these are shortened to the acronym TIMPE – time, income, mobility, population, education.

- *Time*: participants must have a certain amount of leisure time, or time free from work (see Chapter 1), in order to be able to participate in sport or leisure activities. For some, time is not available for leisure, and so this is a constraint on the ability to participate.
- *Income*: the choice and amount of leisure is often closely linked to income, and the ability to pay. Higher income groups of people are likely to have more disposable income to spend on leisure, and so have a greater choice of pastimes. Yet, even low-cost activities such as jogging and walking have higher participation rates among higher income groups. This suggests a link between income and leisure time.
- *Mobility*: this is the ability to access leisure activities. Again, higher income groups tend to be more mobile, and hence have more access to leisure. Less mobile individuals are therefore more likely to base their leisure time around home-based activities (watching television, reading, etc.).
- *Population*: the attitudes and values of people are seen as enabling or inhibiting factors in terms of leisure choice. Very often, people will participate in similar activities to their peers, or others in their income category.
- *Education*: research has shown that with greater levels of education, people also tend to participate to a greater extent.

These factors are not constant, but continually change over time. Yet, very often, it is the lower income groups who tend to be more constrained in their leisure activities. As a result, provision for these groups at the grass-roots level has been a priority in MEDCs in particular, but is now also beginning to be seen as a priority in LEDCs.

CASE STUDY: SPORTS ACTION ZONES, UK

In the UK, the government has for many years had a policy of 'sport for all', trying to allow the entire population, no matter what their situation, the opportunity to participate in sport. Over the years this has taken several forms, usually revolving around local authority provision of specific facilities in line with govern-

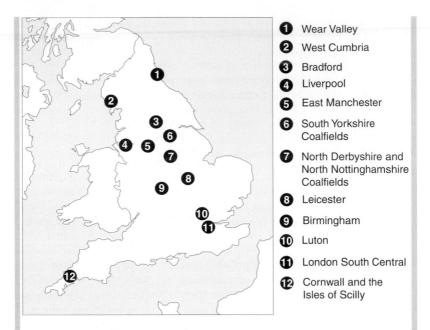

1 Wear Valley
2 West Cumbria
3 Bradford
4 Liverpool
5 East Manchester
6 South Yorkshire Coalfields
7 North Derbyshire and North Nottinghamshire Coalfields
8 Leicester
9 Birmingham
10 Luton
11 London South Central
12 Cornwall and the Isles of Scilly

Figure 45   Sport Action Zones set up around the UK.

ment objectives. The current plan, known as Sport Action Zones (SAZs), was launched in January 2000 as part of the Sport England Lottery Strategy. These zones are relatively evenly spread around the country, and vary in size from whole counties to individual local wards. Included are areas that have experienced economic decline, deprived rural areas and areas of inner-city deprivation (see Figure 45).

The aim of SAZs is "… to address sporting deprivation in some of the most socially and economically deprived areas of the country" (www.archive.sportengland.org). The idea of them is to bring the benefits of sport and physical activity to people who often do not have the opportunity to participate, perhaps due to the influence of one or more of the TIMPE factors. Examples of the types of work the zones carry out are:

- working with young people involved in anti-social behaviour
- working with community health services to support people in poor health
- making local sports centres more accessible
- working with local community groups; in particular, ethnic minorities.

The result of these initiatives is to attempt to tackle areas with social problems, and to increase the access to sports activities for the wider population. This then also attempts to deal with social exclusion, where specific groups of people, for whatever reason, are not participating in sport.

Cornwall and the Isles of Scilly SAZ

Cornwall and the Isles of Scilly were identified as areas requiring a SAZ owing to the fact that several regions within the area had social and economic problems. These areas were easily identifiable using the government's index of multiple deprivation (IMD). The IMD is the official measure of poverty and deprivation in England (see Figure 46).

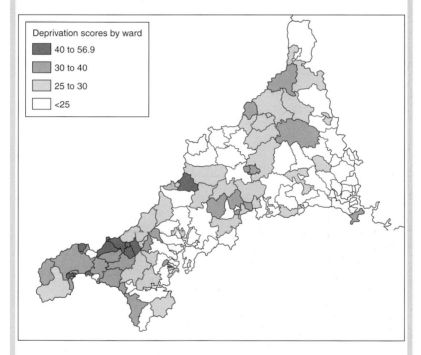

Figure 46   Index of multiple deprivation as applied to Cornwall.

For each area, a range of data is collected to describe living conditions in that area. The index is based on 33 indicators that are classified into several 'domains', each covering a different aspect of deprivation (i.e. employment, health, education, housing, geographical access to services). This creates a score that can then be used to identify areas that are in particular need of attention (see Figure 47).

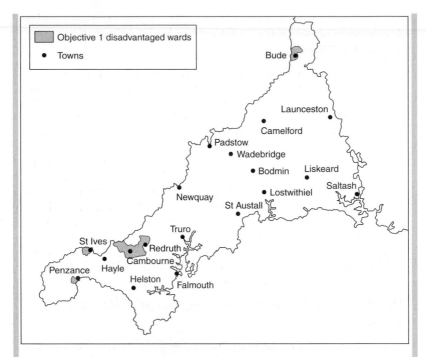

Figure 47 Priority areas identified in Cornwall.

The maps in Figures 46 and 47 indicate that there are several areas requiring immediate attention as far as providing access to sporting opportunities is concerned. For example, Redruth, an area that has had a growing problem with unemployment, has been identified as a priority area on the basis of its IMD score. Unemployment has increased with the decline of tin mining and, as a result, many people will be disadvantaged, and the identification of the areas where these people live has meant that specific actions can be targeted at them to improve their sporting experiences.

The idea of being able to promote and sustain interest in sport has a value, particularly in a society that is becoming increasingly obese and sedentary. The disadvantaged identified in the SAZs are those most likely to miss out on the social, health and educational benefits that sport can bring.

CASE STUDY: LEDC – COMMUNITY SPORTS PROGRAMMES

As has already been stated, sport in LEDCs is often less of a priority, particularly when compared to the need to work for survival. In many countries it has been neglected in deference to schemes to encourage economic growth, and, as a result, schools and communities have been seen to be providing few, if any, sporting opportunities.

Yet, there are several organisations committed to re-establishing sport as an integral part of daily life for people living in LEDCs. Examples of these are the UN Environment Programme (UNEP), EduSport and the Global Sports Alliance (GSA). They each approach the issue of sporting participation in different ways, but their main aim is the same – to promote sport as an important part of life for the whole world, not just for those in MEDCs who have more money and time to be able to participate.

UNEP: 'Nature and Sports Training Camps' – Nairobi, Kenya

UNEP launched this initiative in August 2001 in association with the GSA, in an attempt to combine sports participation such as basketball, tennis and soccer with environmental projects designed to educate children about issues such as recycling and afforestation. According to Klaus Toepfer, Executive Director of UNEP: "Sport can bring out the best in children and young people as they forget about their social status, cultural or linguistic backgrounds".

The project gives thousands of children at any one time the opportunity to participate in sport, and at the same time learn about sustainability through community projects of recycling and tree planting. Another initiative, 'Play for the Planet', also took place in Nairobi in March 2003, involving 4000 children in sporting activities, relating them to environmental projects (www.unep.org). Other projects have taken place throughout Kenya – in Kisumu (April 2002 and 2003) and Mombasa (December 2003), all in a similar vein, and with similar take-up in terms of numbers of children.

Global Sports Alliance: one billion awareness project

The GSA, a Japanese non-profit organisation established in 1999, is dedicated to the creation of a sustainable society and environmentally aware sports cultures. It has set up several initiatives

108 Sporting Futures

(one of which was the Nature and Sports Training Camps) that aim to increase awareness and sustainability through sport:

*   The 'One Billion Awareness' project aims to unite one billion sports enthusiasts around the world in the creation of a new, cleaner and greener society (www.gsa.or.jp).
*   The EcoFlag project is another grass-roots project aimed specifically at increasing environmental awareness through sport (www. ecoflag.com).
*   G-ForSE project aims to promote sustainability and participation opportunities through the efforts of international celebrity matches, and Dream Camps for children in LEDCs (www.g-forse.org).
*   Sports Goods Recycling aims to reduce, reuse and recycle (the 3Rs) sports equipment, and so decrease mass consumption and waste throughout the world.

EduSport: education through sport, Zambia

EduSport is an initiative in Zambia that aims to improve the environment through sporting participation. In a similar way to the UNEP 'Nature and Sports Training Camps', children participate in sporting activities and then learn about the importance of maintaining the environment. Each child is encouraged to educate their peers, and plant at least one tree in their yard (www.edusport.org.zm).

These sporting initiatives are perfect ways for disadvantaged LEDC children to participate in sport, as they provide them with opportunities as well as broaden their education into environmental matters. Yet, it is very much a piecemeal approach at the moment. Sustainability in sports is a message that is clearly reaching some LEDCs, but it can certainly be argued that, as yet, MEDCs have not taken up the challenge of sustainability in sport, neither in terms of developments nor in terms of participation.

SUMMARY

*   Globalisation is an on-going process that can be traced back over 500 years.
*   The current trend in globalisation is one where companies are growing ever bigger and more influential, perhaps at the expense of the less well off.
*   The media has played an enormous part in the globalisation process in relation to sports, but it has not always been beneficial.

- Some sporting organisations such as, Manchester United, have benefited from media intervention, while others have been placed in financial difficulty.
- Globalisation has perpetuated, and possibly even expanded, outmoded and unethical working practices in sports goods manufacturing, such as the use of child labour.
- Sustainable sports development is most easily attainable when provided for at the grass-roots level.
- People in both LEDCs and MEDCs are constrained in their sports and leisure activities by TIMPE factors (time, income, mobility, population, education).
- MEDC and LEDC provision for the disadvantaged requires small-scale, locally planned initiatives that provide knock-on benefits such as health and environmental awareness.

Questions

1. Using Figure 36 as a basis, attempt to draw up a detailed timeline of examples for the globalisation process in relation to sport and leisure.
2. What has been the impact of globalisation on any one Premiership football club, both in terms of the media, marketing and overseas players on it?
3. Using the TIMPE factors as a guide, how does a sport or leisure facility you have studied improve and increase the amount of participation for disadvantaged groups, in order to combat social exclusion?
4. Compare the approaches of two different SAZs in the UK. Which do you think has been the more effective, and why?

Further Reading

These books should be readily available either to buy, or in most academic libraries. While it is by no means an exhaustive list, it serves as a good starting point for research into sport and leisure.

Bale, J. 2003. *Sports Geography*. London: Routledge.
Bale, J. 2000. *Changing Geography – Sportscapes*. Sheffield: Geographical Association.
Bale, J. 1982. *Sport and Place – A Geography of Sport in England, Scotland and Wales*. London: Hurst & Co.
Bale, J. and J. Sang. 1996. *Kenyan Running: Movement Culture, Geography and Global Change*. London: Frank Cass.
Davis, B. *et al*. 1997. *Physical Education and the Study of Sport*. Mosby.
Dunning, E. 1999. *Sport Matters*. London: Routledge.
Gratton, C. and P. Taylor. 2000. *Economics of Sport and Recreation*. London: E & FN Spon.
Haywood, L. *et al*. 1995. *Understanding Leisure*. Nelson Thornes.
Horne *et al*. 1999. *Understanding Sport*. E & FN Spon.
Maguire, J. 1999. *Global Sport – Identities, Societies, Civilisations*. Cambridge: Polity Press.
McIntosh, P. 1987. *Sport in Society*. West London Press.
Prosser, R. 2000. *Leisure, Recreation and Tourism*. London: Collins.
Standeven, J. and P. De Knop. 1999. *Sport Tourism*. Leeds: Human Kinetics.
Torkildsen, G. 1992. *Leisure and Recreation Management*. London: E & FN Spon.
Tribe, J. 2000. *The Economics of Leisure and Tourism*. Oxford: Butterworth-Heinemann.
Witherick, M. and Warn, S. 2003. *The Geography of Sport and Leisure*. Cheltenham: Nelson Thornes.

Useful Websites

Although these websites were correct at the time of writing, because of the nature of the Internet, some may have moved, or may no longer exist. However, they are the main portals, within which there are links to many other excellent resources.

www.archive.sportengland.org
www.arsenal.com
www.bbc.co.uk

www.birmingham.gov.uk
www.caa.org.au/campaigns/nike
www.cnp.org.uk – each UK National Park also has its own website,
all worth a visit
www.commonwealthgames.com
www.footballculture.net
www.games-legacy.com
www.g-forse.org
www.ghs.gov.uk
www.google.co.uk (*tip* – type your search in between double quotation marks – that way the search engine will look for the phrase,
rather than individual words).
www.labourbehindthelabel.org
www.manchester.gov.uk
www.manutd.com
www.mediaguardian.co.uk
www.olympic.org
www.play-the-game.org
www.resource.gov.uk
www.sportactionzone.org.uk
www.sportdevelopment.org.uk
www.sportengland.org
www.sporting-goods-industry.com
www.statistics.gov.uk
www.swansea.gov.uk
www.undp.org
www.unep.org
www.unesco.org

References

Andreff, W. 2003. Sport and Development Paper Presented to 1st
International Association of Sports Economists Workshop – 6–7
February, Brive, France. http://users.pullman.com/rodfort/IASE/
Bulletins/BulletinNo6-3-03.doc
Andreff, W. 2000. Sport and Economic Development. www.play-the-
game.org
Bale, J. 1990. In the shadow of the stadium: football grounds as urban
nuisances. *Geography* **75**(4): 324–34.
Barsby, J. 2002. Kenyan runners: are they born or made? *Marathon
News*. Race Entry Issue: 34–5.
Born, M. 2003. 14 m tune in for moment of truth. *Daily Telegraph*, 26
November.
Case, R. 2003. Greenfield versus brownfield sites for sports stadia – a
tale from Southampton. *Geo Factsheet* 149.

Conn, D. 2003. Residents vow to battle on over Arsenal's new home. *Independent,* 20 December.

Coalter, F., C. MacGregor and R. Denham. 1996. *Visitors to National Parks.* Cheltenham: Countryside Commission.

Council of Europe. 1992. *European Sports Charter.* Council of Europe.

Countryside Commission. 1992. *Trends in Transport in the Countryside.* Cheltenham: Countryside Commission.

Darby, P. 2001. African footballers migration to europe. *Global Issues* 10. www.belfast.org/globalisation/africanfootball.htm

Ekpo, K. 1991. Socio-cultural views of leisure in a multi-tribal setting *World Leisure and Recreation Association.* Summer: 13–16.

Digby, B. (ed.) 2000. *Changing Environments.* Oxford: Heinemann

Gee, N. 2002. Second homes in England and Wales. *Geography Review* **15**(5): 30–33.

Guinness, P. 2002. *Access to Geography: Migration.* London: Hodder & Stoughton.

House of Commons Environment Committee. 1995. *The Environmental Impact of Leisure Activities.* London: HMSO.

Hudson, R. 1997. Tourism, leisure and regeneration in northeast England. *Geography Review* **10**(3): 18–19.

Jones, C. 1998. UK National Parks – tourism in Grasmere. *Geography Review* **11**(5): 2–6.

Jones, P. and D. Hillier 1997. Changes brewing: superpub developments in the UK. *Geography Review* **10**(3): 26–28.

Law, C. 2001. *Discovering Cities: Manchester.* Sheffield: Geographical Association.

Lean, G. 2000. A gold medal for being green. *Independent,* 6 August.

Lyon, J. 2000. *Maldives.* Victoria: Lonely Planet Publications.

Manley, I. 1991. *Tourism and the Environment – Maintaining the Balance.* English Tourist Board.

Newcastle Gateshead Initiative. 1999. *Leisure and Pleasure – Newcastle/ Gateshead.* Newcastle: Newcastle Gateshead Initiative Brochure.

Rennie, D. 2001. China spins its way to Olympic triumph. *Daily Telegraph,* 14 July.

Ricci, F. 2000. *African Football Yearbook 2000.* Rome: Ricci.

Robertson, R. 1992. *Globalization: Social Theory and Global Culture.* London: Sage.

Skari, T. 2003. A run for the money. *Time Europe Magazine,* 8 September. www.time.com/time/europe.html

Smith, D. 1996. Atlanta: inequality and injustice in the Olympic City. *Geography Review* **10**(1): 2–5.

Speake, J. and V. Fox. 2002. *Regenerating City Centres.* Sheffield: Geographical Association.

Tanser, T. 1997. *Train Hard, Win Easy: The Kenyan Way.* Mountain View: Tafnews.

TED. 1998. *Golf and the Environment.* London: Tourism Concern.

Terrell, S. 2000. An investigation into the concept of 'quiet areas' and their management within the National Parks of England and Wales. University of Birmingham thesis.

Westall, A., P. Ramsden and N. Foley 2001. *Micro-entrepreneurs: Creating Enterprising Societies.* London: IPPR/NEF.

Whannel, G. 1992. *Fields in Vision: Television Sport and Cultural Transformation.* London: Routledge.

Whitson, D. 1998. Circuits of promotion: media, marketing and the globalization of sport. In *Media Sport* edited by Wenner, L., pp. 57–72. London: Routledge.

Williams, R. 2003. Cherono wins under another name and flag. *The Guardian* 27 August. http://sport.guardian.co.uk/athletics

Website References

Although these websites were correct at the time of writing, because of the nature of the Internet, some may have moved, or may no longer exist.

http://jalandhar.nic.in/html/sports_goods_industry.htm
http://politics.guardian.co.uk/localgovernment
http://sunset.swan.ac.uk/swantour
http://theworkfoundation.co.uk
http://ucatlas.ucsc.edu/gdp/gdpmap.html
www2.umist.ac.uk/sport/2_art2.htm
www.chinahotelsite.com/city/beijing_2008_olympic.gif
www.copelandbc.gov.uk
www.ecoflag.com
www.edusport.org.zm
www.gamesbids.com/english/archives/former2008.shtml
www.gsa.or.jp
www.hunttech.com/sgepc/profile.htm
www.interstate.co.uk/arsenalworld/forsale/021297.htm
www.msu.edu/course/prr/Russell,ch5.doc
www.msu.edu/course/prr/RussellChapter5part2.doc
www.ofcom.org.uk – ITC Report 2002
www.palgrave.com/sociology/pdfs/chap18.pdf
www.ralph.swan.ac.uk/swantour
www.reefrelief.org
www.s-cool.co.uk (Bristol Case Study)
www.saccsweb.org
www.sadili.com/sportscamps.html
www.sln.org.uk
www.sportdevelopment.org.uk/downloads/impact_of_games_Apr02.
   pdf

www.sportdevelopment.org.uk/downloads/research/M2002_base-
line_2001.pdf
www.swansea.gov.uk/aboutswansea/historic.htm
www.swansea.gov.uk/devplan
www.themovechannel.com/sitefeatures/news/2002-may/24b.asp
www.tierramerica.org/english/2002/117/1acentos2.shtml
www.transport2000.org.uk/goodpractice/Birmingham.htm
www.usatoday.com/sports/olympics

Index